GHOSTHUNTING
FLORIDA

T0165695

AMERICA'S

HAUNTED ROAD TRIP

Titles in the *America's Haunted Road Trip* Series:

GHOSTHUNTING FLORIDA

DAVE LAPHAM

CLERISY PRESS

Ghosthunting Florida

Published by Clerisy Press
Distributed by Publishers Group West
Printed in the United States of America
First edition 2010

Library of Congress Cataloging-in-Publication Data

Lapham, Dave, 1939–
  Ghosthunting Florida / Dave Lapham.
  p. cm.

  ISBN-13: 978-1-57860-450-0 (pbk.); ISBN-10: 1-57860-450-8 (pbk.)
  ISBN 978-1-57860-451-7 (ebook); ISBN 978-1-57860-589-7 (hardcover)

  1. Haunted places—Florida. 2. Ghosts—Florida. I. Title.

  BF1472.U6L373 2010
  133.109759—dc22

                                        2010020569

Editor: John Kachuba
Cover design: Scott McGrew
Cover and interior photos provided by Dave Lapham
  unless otherwise credited.

Clerisy Press
An imprint of AdventureKEEN
306 Greenup Street
Covington, KY 41101
www.clerisypress.com

TABLE OF CONTENTS

THE PANHANDLE 171

Welcome to America's Haunted Road Trip

Do you believe in ghosts?

If you are like 52 percent of Americans (according to a recent Harris Poll), you do believe that ghosts walk among us. Perhaps you have heard your name called in a dark and empty house. It could be that you have awoken to the sound of footsteps outside your bedroom door, only to find no one there. It is possible that you saw your grandmother sitting in her favorite rocker chair, the same grandmother who had passed away several years before. Maybe you took a photo of a crumbling, deserted farmhouse and discovered strange mists and orbs in the photo, anomalies that were not visible to your naked eye.

If you have experienced similar paranormal events, then you know that ghosts exist. Even if you have not yet experienced these things, you are curious about the paranormal world, the spirit realm. If you weren't, you would not now be reading this Preface to the latest book in the *America's Haunted Road Trip* series from Clerisy Press.

Over the last several years, I have investigated haunted locations across the country and with each new site, I found myself becoming more fascinated with ghosts. What are they? How do they manifest themselves? Why are they here? These are just a few of the questions I have been asking. No doubt, you have been asking the same questions.

The books in the *America's Haunted Road Trip* series can help you find the answers to your questions about ghosts. We've gathered together some of America's top ghost writers (no pun intended) and researchers and asked them to write about their states' favorite haunts. Each location that they write about is open to the public so that you can visit them for yourself and try out your ghosthunting skills. In addition to telling you about their often hair-raising adventures, the writers have included maps and travel directions so that you can take your own haunted road trip.

People may think that Florida is all about Mickey Mouse, but Dave Lapham's *Ghosthunting Florida* proves that the state is fertile ground for entities even more fantastic than a talking mouse. The book is a spine-tingling trip through Florida's small towns and lively cities, its historic sites and fun spots, all of them haunted. Ride shotgun with Dave as he seeks out Civil War ghosts at the Olustee Battlefield and the spirits of Spanish soldiers at St. Augustine's Spanish Military Hospital. Travel with him to the Audubon House in Key West where the ghosts of several children killed by yellow fever still roam the house in which they once played; if you're lucky—or perhaps, unlucky—you will find the missing Demon Doll. And who, or what, is heard pacing the upstairs hallway of Monticello's Palmer House? Hang on tight; *Ghosthunting Florida* is a scary ride.

But once you've finished reading this book, don't unbuckle your seatbelt. There are still forty-nine states left for your haunted road trip! See you on the road!

John Kachuba
Editor, America's Haunted Road Trip

Introduction

After having published *Ghosts of St. Augustine* (Pineapple Press, 1997) and *Ancient City Hauntings* (Pineapple Press, 2004), I thought I was finished with ghosts for a while, but they weren't finished with me. Out of the blue, I was given an opportunity to write *Ghosthunting Florida,* covering the whole state. I immediately jumped at the chance, and now my ghosts and I are back in business.

My interest in ghosts and the inexplicable events we all encounter during our lives has been casual but persistent. I am as sensitive to the paranormal as a bull gator, but I have had many, many experiences that have mystified me and that I cannot explain. And I have so many questions. What are ghosts really? And exactly, physically, where is "the other side," or Heaven, or whatever you may call it? And why do some ghosts stick around and others don't? And clothes! Those who see ghosts, apparitions, almost always see them dressed in period clothes. Clothes are inanimate, so how can they be transported to the afterlife?

And why doesn't everyone believe in ghosts? There are volumes of research that make it pretty clear to me that the death of the physical body is not the end, and yet so many still deny the existence of an afterlife. Deborah Blum in her excellent book, *Ghost Hunters* (Penguin Books, 2006), examines the studies conducted by William James, brother of author Henry James, and a group of highly respected scientists during the nineteenth century. Their studies were meant to bring understanding of life after death and to bridge the gulf between science and faith, to make psychic research a legitimate branch of science. Still, there are skeptics.

Ghosthunting Florida, along with the other books in the America's Haunted Road Trip series, seeks to answer some of these questions and to sway skeptics with accurate, objective observations and experiences, and then let the reader draw their own conclusions. Whether you're a paranormal investigator, an amateur ghosthunter, or just someone who enjoys a good ghost story, you will like this book and find it useful. In addition to the stories, which I have arranged by region, I have included a ghosthunting travel guide, Visiting Haunted Places, which provides detailed information about visiting the sites written about in this book and a list of resources.

For those who might wish to do their own ghost hunting, here are some guidelines and rules of etiquette:

1. Conduct all your investigations with an open mind and don't be fooled by the "evidence." No one has yet proven scientifically beyond a doubt that ghosts actually exist. You probably won't be the one to do it, so be non-judgmental and open about what you experience and observe. And be skeptical of the evidence you gather by examining all possible explanations.

2. Interview witnesses separately, so that they don't influence each other with their testimony.

3. Document all your activities. When professional and serious paranormal investigators visit sites, they are often loaded with infrared cameras, EMF meters, and all manner of highly sensitive equipment. If you have that sort of equipment, by all means use it. I don't, but I like to carry a pen and notebook, a tape recorder, and a camera. It is helpful if each member of your party carries the same equipment also. The tape recorder is good

for recording interviews, and you might catch unidentifiable sounds or voices from a site.

The camera is a great tool, too. You might be surprised by what you pick up with your camera that you can't see with your eyes. Most often bright, white spots—orbs—will appear. They can often be attributed to reflections, dust particles, water spots, and the like, but sometimes, when you enlarge these photos there seems to be no explanation for anomalies. Orbs are actually quite common.

4. Respect the site. Respect the history of a haunted site and the people who inhabited it. Take nothing from the site and leave nothing. Do not enter any site without permission and observe the rules and regulations. A special note about cemeteries: Cemeteries are sacred places, and they tend to be very haunted, often by malevolent spirits, so once you get permission to visit a cemetery after hours, don't visit alone and always try to include an experienced person in your group. You should never enter any site without permission. If you obey the rules and use a little common sense, people will be more inclined to help you in your explorations.

5. Respect the privacy of your contacts. Some people may tell you their stories but, for whatever reason, may not want to reveal their identity. Respect their wishes. I used real names in this book, unless permission was not given to do so, in which case I used pseudonyms which I marked with an asterisk (*) after the name.

6. Be a knowledgeable ghosthunter. This is important. Study the literature. Learn from serious ghosthunters and paranormal investigators. We do not know or understand the laws that govern the world of spirits, and

exploring that world is traveling into the unknown. The experts say that the more you know about it, the better your chances of being successful—and of keeping safe. And never, ever resort to dubious psychic "tools," such as Ouija boards, which can, in inexperienced hands, summon unwanted and uncontrollable spirits. I urge you to read and learn from the experts before venturing forth on your own ghosthunting expedition.

As I said, I am not very sensitive. Yes, I have experienced the inexplicable, have been overwhelmed by feelings of negative energy, have seen images that may or may not have been apparitions, but I am no psychic, and I am sure that my imagination had much to do with many of my experiences. But I have sensitive friends, most particularly my sometimes sidekick, Joanne Maio. She doesn't like to be called psychic, but she is extremely sensitive, so much so that she often is asked to walk through buildings and areas suspected of being haunted and give her impressions.

I have divided the state into five geographical regions: The Keys and the South, West Central, East Central, North, and the Panhandle. Each is unique in its own way. Because Florida is such a long state, over one thousand miles from Key West to Pensacola, I would recommend visiting each area separately, taking time to enjoy all the many interesting places in each region. There are many excellent guides to day trips around the state, and ghosthunting activities can easily be incorporated into these excursions, even on extended weekend mini-vacations. In fact, many readers of my previous books have said that they've used the stories as springboards for their children to research and study the history and culture of particular places.

For the avid ghosthunter and paranormal investigator, the Ghostly Resources section in the back of the book provides a listing of online resources, books, and organizations helpful to me in researching the stories. The organizations listed are especially open to assisting others delve into the mysteries of the other side.

I hope you will enjoy *Ghosthunting Florida* and find it useful and entertaining as you conduct your own explorations of the spirit world. Please feel free to contact me through my publisher if you would like to share your experiences. Don't forget to check out the other books in this series; even though you might not be able to visit the sites, the books contain some great stories!

Now, buckle up and join Joanne, my intrepid wife, Sue, and me as we begin ghosthunting Florida.

Dave Lapham
Orlando, Florida

The Keys and the South

Arcadia
  Arcadia's Old Opera House
    & Museum

Delray Beach
  The Colony Hotel & Cabaña Club

Key West
  Audubon House & Tropical
    Gardens
  Captain Tony's Saloon

Hard Rock Café
La Concha
Marrero's Guest Mansion

Miami
  Historic Biltmore Hotel of
    Coral Gables

West Palm Beach
  Riddle House

CHAPTER 1

La Concha
KEY WEST

KEY WEST IS ONE OF MY FAVORITE places and is also very haunted, so I decided to make it my first stop on this road trip of haunted Florida. My wife, Sue, and I drove down for our weeklong visit during the off-season, when it was quieter (better for ghosthunting) and also less expensive.

After we'd checked in and gotten settled, we paid a visit to The Original Key West Ghost Tours. Originally founded by my friend, David Sloan, Brant and Karen Voss now own the tour company and maintain a store of ghostly items in the Crowne Plaza Key West—La Concha.

Better known simply as La Concha or the Conch, it is a Key West landmark. Built in 1926 by Carl Aubuchon as the first "first class hotel" in Key West, with elevators, private baths, marble floors, and all the other amenities of any five-star hotel in the country, it was no surprise that it was an immediate success with wealthy high society. During the 1920s the sponge-gathering, cigar-making, and rum-running industries were booming, and tourists by the hundreds flocked to Key West on Henry Flagler's Overseas Railroad. Key West was the richest city in the United States.

Then came the stock market crash of 1929 followed by the 1935 Labor Day hurricane. Key West, literally cut off from the mainland almost overnight, became the poorest city in America. But the Conch survived, barely, thanks to the beginning of the Second World War, and entertained such celebrities as Ernest Hemingway and Tennessee Williams.

After the war, however, age and competition took their toll on the hotel, and by the 1980s the building was closed and boarded up except for the rooftop bar and a kitchen downstairs to service it. The rooftop and its bar had always been one of the hotel's attractions. With seven floors, the Conch was the tallest building in Key West, and the views from the roof were magnificent.

In 1986, Atlanta architect Richard Rauh, using old blueprints, photographs, interviews with longtime residents, and samples of wallpaper stripped from the walls, renovated the hotel and restored it to its former glory.

Brant was waiting for us at the Ghost Tours office when we arrived. Since we were already there in the La Concha, he took us on a tour, telling us about the history of the place and about the ghosts. The fifth floor is especially active, and patrons have reported seeing a male ghost there quite often. Because Ernest Hemingway stayed on the fifth floor and mentioned the hotel in his novel *To Have and Have Not* (Scribner's, 1937), most people assume the ghost is Ernest Hemingway. But it's not. It is actually Brent Hoekstra.

On New Year's Eve 1982, Brent, a Key West resident, went up to the bar shortly after midnight to meet friends who worked there. They planned to celebrate New Year's Eve down on Duval Street. Brent's friends were still cleaning up when he arrived. Anxious to join the festivities in the street seven stories below, he volunteered to help.

One of his friends was stacking dirty glasses and dishes on a cart to be taken down to the kitchen. When the cart was full Brent offered to run it down for him. His friend handed him the key to the freight elevator and went back to cleaning up. He forgot to tell Brent how the elevator worked.

With passenger elevators today, you simply push the button, the car comes to your floor, the door opens, and you get on. However, with this particular freight elevator, left over from the 1920s, the door did not stay closed until the car reached your level, unlike present-day elevators. When you unlocked the door, it opened. You then had to press the button to bring the elevator car up. Brent didn't know that. He unlocked the door and, pulling the cart behind him, backed into the opening—and plummeted onto the car six floors below. He died instantly. When the hotel reopened in 1986, Brent's ghost was seen hanging around the Hemingway suite on the fifth floor.

Why Brent picked the fifth floor no one knows, but most are certain the spirit there is his. One of his close friends, a security guard at La Concha, often encountered Brent on the fifth floor. Brent's friend was always a bit uncomfortable, but he was never frightened. In fact, waiting for the elevator on that floor, he often felt a comforting hand on his shoulder, as if Brent were telling him he was okay and that the elevator was safe.

There are many other stories of sightings on the fifth floor. One hotel patron said he woke from a deep sleep in the middle of the night feeling as if someone were staring at him from a chair across the room. He jumped out of bed to confront the man, and there was a loud crash, as if a table or heavy chair had tipped over. He flicked on the lights; no one else was in the room, and no furniture had been moved.

The rooftop bar of the La Concha provides not only exquisite views of Key West and its breathtaking sunsets, but also a spectacular diving platform for anyone wishing to commit suicide in a gruesome way. Thirteen people have jumped to their deaths over the years from the La Concha rooftop.

On October 7, 1992, Fred Butner, a well-known local attorney, took the plunge onto Duval Street. His former secretary, Susan, supposedly had reported him to the Florida Bar Association for negligent and illegal practices. Knowing his business and his reputation would be destroyed, he decided to take his own life, but he was vindictive. He was going to ruin Susan while he was at it. He wrote several extortion notes that seemed to come from her and that he carried on his person, and he planted an envelope with payoff money in her car. He even carried a tape recorder with him as he entered the hotel, announcing his arrival on the tape and supposedly telling Susan, "I have what you want." Then, he yelled, "No! No!" and the last sound on the tape recorder was his body hitting the pavement below. A subsequent investigation exonerated Susan.

In 2006, Michael Bachand, a troubled Orlando man, came to Key West and went up to the rooftop for a drink. He ordered a glass of chardonnay and walked outside to a spot overlooking the swimming pool. He drank his wine in a few gulps, set the glass on the wall—and did a half gainer onto the pool deck below, which was also the roof of The Original Key West Ghost Tours store.

Shortly after that, drinking chardonnay at the rooftop bar became a bit of a problem. When someone ordered chardonnay, glasses would often get knocked out of their hands or plastic cups split in half. Down on the pool deck, trays of drinks were often tipped out of servers' hands, but only female servers. Perhaps Mr. Bachand was distraught over a love affair gone sour.

Even more bizarre after this event were the happenings in the Ghost Tour's store. The chandeliers began to rattle, and lights in the store would go out one by one, leaving the place in darkness. A violent wind often blew through, scattering T-shirts and books; doors slammed shut and opened again; and a creepy shadow was occasionally seen wandering throughout the store and up into the ceiling. Things also seemed to occur just outside the store. Brant had parked his truck on Fleming Street in front of the store one evening. As he started to get out, the manually operated windows began going up and down and the doors locking and unlocking. He was able to jump out of the truck, but as he did, the battery exploded, setting the truck on fire.

While these happenings were negative and sometimes violent, there was also a female presence in the store that seemed to be trying to protect everyone. Who this presence was, no one knew.

Eddie Ellington had been a tour guide for the Original Tours for several years. He was uniquely qualified—he was a medium. Because of his gift, when he was in the store, he was intimately aware of everything going on and seemed to be able to quiet much of the negative activity.

Unfortunately, Eddie died in 2008. He had no family but had told Brant that he wanted to be cremated and buried someplace in Key West. When he died, Brant made the arrangements for Eddie's cremation. Afterward, he was given the box of Eddie's ashes and wondered where Eddie would most want to be buried. Then, a thought came to him: why not the store? Eddie's life had revolved around it, and the tours and his presence always seemed to reduce the negative energy and activities. So, that's what Brant did. Eddie now sits on a shelf right behind the counter, keeping watch over everything.

And, truth be told, not much goes on there today. In fact, The Original Key West Ghost Tours store is now a pretty quiet place, but La Concha's fifth floor still remains active—and who knows when some sad soul will take the plunge from the rooftop.

CHAPTER 2

Hard Rock Café
Key West

ADAM "PIERCE" BERG WAS WORKING LATE. He was the maintenance man, and there was always something that needed to be done that he couldn't attend to while customers were there. Tonight he was changing light fixtures in the bar. It was 2:45 A.M., long after the staff had left and over an hour before the cleaning crew came in. He had heard the bizarre stories from bartender Niki Padron and others, so he was a little uncomfortable about being alone in this old house. But Pierce was more worried about all the revelers outside on the street. He didn't want to be disturbed, so he locked himself in and activated the security system.

He was screwing in a bracket when he heard a noise, or

thought he did. He stopped and listened. Someone was whistling, and the whistler seemed to be in the bar on the far side
of the room. Pierce's spine began to tingle, and goose bumps
formed on his arms. Frightened, he yelled out, "Knock that crap
off!" The whistling stopped.

Pierce went back to work, a little shaken, but moments
later he heard footsteps on the front stairs just outside the bar.
The whistling started again from the same area. Completely
unnerved, Pierce grabbed his tools and raced out the front door
without even turning off the security system. The alarm blasted
the quiet of the early morning. A police patrol just happened to
be passing down Duval Street and immediately flipped on its
emergency lights. The officers nabbed a shaking Pierce before
he even got to the street.

Pierce still works at the Hard Rock Café. He's a waiter now
and doesn't do maintenance anymore. He refuses to work after
hours.

When it comes to paranormal events, Key West's Hard Rock
Café is an active place. Mandy Dunn, the sales and marketing
manager, was in the third floor office one evening about ten,
working on reports. The bar and dining areas downstairs were
still crowded with patrons. As she worked, someone began whistling a little tune over and over. The whistler was very close.
She knew no one else was up there, but she called out, "Who's
there?" No one answered, but the whistling stopped. Curious,
she checked the security cameras covering the third floor. She
was the only one captured on film.

Niki Padron often sees shadows moving around the bar area
while she is cleaning up after closing time. Glasses move along
the bar. Chairs and stools move by themselves with footsteps
usually accompanying this activity.

My wife, Sue, and I visited the Hard Rock midday when business was slow. Don Estep, the general manager, gave us a tour

and told us a lot about the building. William Curry had come to Key West from the Bahamas in 1847 as a small boy. His family was penniless when they arrived in Key West, but William had become the island's first millionaire, making his fortune salvaging shipwrecks in the pirate-infested waters around the Keys. He died in 1896, the richest man in Florida. He had married and had a family, and in 1888 built what was to eventually become the Hard Rock Café for his son, Robert, as a wedding gift. The original house had fifteen to eighteen rooms—no one is quite sure—and a basement, which was unusual for Florida, especially Key West. None of the staff likes to go into the basement, now used only for storage.

Legend says that Robert fell on hard times through bad investments, gambling, and bad luck. After his wife and family left him, he hanged himself in what was the bathroom of the master suite on the second floor, part of which is now the ladies' restroom. Women customers have reported stall and entry doors opening and closing, whistling, footsteps, and even taps on the shoulder as they walked down the hall.

One manager kept seeing a man walking up the stairs and into the wall at the top landing. He saw items moving around the bar. He heard footsteps, whistling, and other strange noises. Unable to cope with all of these unearthly goings-on, he invited a priest in to bless the entire establishment, room by room, with holy water. It had no effect. The activity continued, and the manager left shortly thereafter.

Many paranormal investigators have gone through the building, and it has appeared several times on television, including the Discovery Channel and the Travel Channel's "America's Most Haunted Restaurants." A psychic who flew in for the Discovery Channel's investigation came directly from the airport. She had never been to Key West before and knew nothing about the history of the Hard Rock Café. As she walked through, she did, indeed, discover the man upstairs. She felt that he was the one walking around the house, whistling, and tapping people on their shoulders. But she also found a little girl brushing her hair in the upstairs restroom and, just as puzzling, a woman and a small girl by the fireplace downstairs. She said that the reason there was so much activity after Hard Rock's closing time was because the period between when the staff left and the cleaning crew came in was the only time the "family" could enjoy the house.

Don Estep was surprised when he learned this; no one had ever reported the woman and the two girls. Who were they? Could they have been Robert Curry's family? And if they were, what had happened to them? Could they have all died there? If they had, why was there no historical evidence of that?

Sue and I paid a visit to Tom Hambright, the Marion County Library historian and a decades-long resident of Key West. He had some interesting things to tell us. The Key West Order of Elks purchased the Curry house in 1920, and it was the Elks Club until the mid-1960s. Then it was The Shell Man, a shop selling seashells, and Mario City, an Italian restaurant, among others. It also sat vacant from time to time.

Mr. Hambright had dozens of stories to tell us about Key West, and the many tales about the Curry House only added to its mystery. He had evidence that Robert Curry actually died in a New York hospital. He also pointed out that, although the legends say that Curry hanged himself from rafters in the second floor bathroom, there probably were no open beams or exposed rafters there as this was an expensive Victorian mansion. So, even if Robert Curry did hang himself in the house, he probably didn't do it on the second floor but in the attic above.

He also told us about a visitor to the Elks' Club who shot himself in the bathtub of the upstairs bathroom, ostensibly to contain the mess. Is the ghost of this stranger the whistler, the specter who walks through walls, the spirit who walks around and taps people on their shoulders?

There was also the information concerning a young divorcee with a somewhat tarnished reputation. The Elks often held dances in a large banquet room in the rear of the building. On one particular evening, the young lady was there dancing and flirting with as many men as she could. One minute she was on the dance floor, the center of attention, and the next she had vanished. No one saw her leave, and no one saw with whom she left. Several years later, her bones were found and identified on Saddlebunch Key, a small island to the north. The case, presumably a murder, was never solved. Could this nameless woman be haunting the house, sitting in front of the fireplace?

Mr. Hambright also knew people who had inexplicable experiences at the Elks Club. He had a friend in the early 1960s who tended bar there and often invited friends over in the late evening for a nightcap when the club was closing. He confessed that he was afraid to be in the place alone after hours because of all the strange noises he had heard.

The Elks Club maintenance man, another friend of Mr. Hambright's, also had many unexplained experiences there. Once he was cleaning up on the first floor when he heard a loud crash upstairs. He raced up to see what had happened. A large, heavy table had been tipped over. He got frightened and turned on all the lights. He even went up to the attic, but the door was locked, and he knew no one could be up there. He checked the whole place—both the first and second floors and even the basement—and turned on every light. There wasn't a soul in the place. Pretty frightening. He started packing up to go; that's when he heard footsteps from the second or maybe the third floor attic. He'd had enough and rushed out.

Sue and I went back to the Hard Rock Café later that evening. We couldn't stay up until two A.M., but it was close to midnight. Since it was mid-week, few people were around. Mr. Estep escorted us through the house again, even going into the basement. I had to agree—the basement was definitely a spooky place. We walked slowly through the main floor, then up to the second, and finally up to the third-floor offices. I even went into the ladies' room on the second floor.

Unfortunately, neither of us had any experiences, except for some eerie feelings and temperature changes, all probably brought on by the stories we had heard. I only wished I had had my ghost magnet friend, Joanne, with me. I'm sure she would have sensed all the paranormal activity around us.

CHAPTER 3

Captain Tony's Saloon
KEY WEST

CAPTAIN TONY'S SALOON on Greene Street is shrouded in myth and mystery. According to local lore, it was constructed in 1852 and was an icehouse, which doubled as the city morgue. In 1898 it supposedly housed the Navy's Naval Radio Station and reported the sinking of the USS *Maine* around the world. By 1912 it became home to a cigar factory and a few years later to a bordello and bar. When Prohibition shut down the bars and gin mills across the country, several different speakeasies occupied the building. As one was closed by the authorities, another soon opened up—the last being The Blind Pig, which specialized in bootleg rum, gambling, and prostitutes.

When the Prohibition Act was repealed in 1933, Josie Russell rented it and opened Sloppy Joe's Bar. Ernest Hemingway spent many evenings there between 1933 and 1937, drinking with his friends. When the landlord raised the rent by a dollar in 1938, Russell moved around the corner on Duval Street, and the bar passed through several hands under various names.

In 1958 Captain Tony Tarracino, a charter-boat captain and the archetypical "Conch," bought the bar and christened it Captain Tony's Saloon. Tony owned the bar until 1989, when he sold it to run for mayor of Key West, but he was always a frequent visitor there until his death in November 2008.

The stories about Captain Tony's Saloon are legion.

When the place was supposedly a morgue, bodies of unidentified people or those too poor to pay for a funeral were buried right next door where a pool table stands now. At some point when the area was just an open piece of land, a hurricane blew through, and the resulting water caused many of the bones to rise to the surface. Captain Tony decided to make a small cemetery and give them a decent reburial. Since so many of the residents of Key West were Bahamians and voodoo and Santeria practitioners—and staunch believers in ghosts—he had a small stone wall built around the area with bottles of holy water interspersed throughout it.

And there is the story of Reba Sawyer. Married, she had a long-term affair with a married man. They used to meet at the bar, knowing neither of their spouses would likely come near the place. She died in 1950. Her husband discovered her infidelity a few years later while going through some of her old letters and showed up at the bar one evening with a small tombstone that read "Reba Sawyer 1900–1950." He had taken it from the Key West cemetery. He dropped it on the sidewalk outside and said, "Here. She liked to hang out at this place so much, she might as well stay." Captain Tony brought the tombstone inside

the saloon, where it still rests. Captain Tony didn't want to leave
Reba out on the sidewalk.

There is also Elvira. Her flat tombstone is part of the south
floor of the building and reads:

> "Elvira
> Daughter of Joseph & Susannah Edmunds
> Died Dec 21 1822
> Ag'd 19yrs 8 Mos & 21 Days."

Was this area a cemetery in 1822? No one knows.

A large tree grows in the middle of the bar area, which used
to be an open patio. Legend says that a local woman murdered
her husband and children one night and cut them into pieces.
The residents of Key West were fairly openminded about almost
anything. Some even figured that the woman's husband deserved
it, but they drew the line with murdering children. So a lynch
mob seized her right from her bed—she was wearing only a blue
nightgown—took her downtown to what served as the lynching
tree, and hanged her.

A hangman's noose is made with a large knot, which serves
both to form a loop and also to break the prisoner's neck. If the
knot doesn't do its job, the prisoner strangles to death, his or
her face turning blue in the process. It was reported that is what
happened to the "Lady in Blue." The knot did not break her neck;
she strangled to death.

Captain Tony was married three times and had thirteen children. He was said to have been a caring father and husband. But
he always liked to keep his options open and maintained a residence for entertaining his various girlfriends above the saloon,
accessible only through a ship's hatch in the ceiling at the back
of the bar. One night he heard the iron gate to the patio swing
open and then close. He ran down to see who it was. No one was
there. The next night the same thing happened. Again, no one

was there. Tony had had enough. He figured someone had the key, so after the bar closed, he left his current paramour and sat in the patio behind the tree with the lights off.

The first few nights nothing happened. Then one evening he heard the gate creak open and looked around the tree. He was stunned to see a woman in a nightgown with a blue cast surrounding her. She walked right to the tree and disappeared through it. Captain Tony related the tale often in the years to come.

Tom Hambright, the Marion County Library historian, has some other ideas about these stories. In the first place, he doubts that Key West ever had a morgue until recent times, although there might have been some place used as a makeshift morgue during natural disasters or epidemics. When people died, they were usually prepared for burial right in their own homes and put in the ground fairly quickly, considering the heat and humidity of Key West. Having a hanging tree next to the morgue might also have been convenient, but there was a gallows at the courthouse, which a lynch mob may or may not have used.

He also questions the icehouse theory. It is doubtful that the building was used as an icehouse. Its walls are too thin, and there is sufficient evidence that the Shell Warehouse, which has thick stone walls, was probably the icehouse.

The date of the building is also debatable. There may have been something on the site in 1852, but there is strong evidence against that date. In 1905 Mr. Dee Forest built the Key West Naval Radio Station, the first in a chain of U. S. Navy communications stations extending from Cape Elizabeth, Maine, to New Orleans. Shortly after, he decided to compete with Western Union and built his own civilian radio-telegraph station on the site where Captain Tony's is now located. He used the tree there as a base for his antenna.

What about Elvira? Captain Tony was a very kind and considerate person, even if he was promiscuous and eccentric. He loved to tell a good story, and he made up a lot of them about the saloon. If a story went over and interested people, he'd keep embellishing it, dragging it out as long as possible. After all, if people were in his bar listening to his stories, they also were drinking. It was good for business.

Allegedly, Tony found bones in a dry well next to the saloon. No one could identify them, of course. He felt sorry for whoever it was, so he made up a name, Elvira Edmunds, buried her in the bar, and put in the stone, believing that, whoever she was, she deserved to be remembered. No one knows for sure whether there is actually a body in the grave or not.

The same is true for Reba Sawyer and for the skeleton behind the bar, supposedly pieced together from three separate skeletons from the "graveyard" under the south floor. No one knows for sure.

Still, the saloon is no doubt haunted. Anita Pierce works at the bar and says that the pool room, which is located over an old cistern, is especially eerie. She won't go in there by herself, nor will Trent Binder, a balladeer who performs at Captain Tony's regularly.

One of Anita's friends used to date the bar manager and would wait for him there while he closed up at night. One night she was sitting at the bar while he went "up the hatch" to lock up the evening's receipts. After a few minutes, she thought she saw him come down and go directly into the women's restroom. A moment later, he came down from upstairs again.

"How did you do that?" she asked.

"Do what?"

"A minute ago I saw you come down the stairs and go into the ladies' room."

"You're crazy," he replied. "I just came down from upstairs."

They both went over to the ladies' room. They could see light under the door and they called out. No one answered. Hard as they tried, they couldn't get the door open, although they could see that the locking bolt was not in place. A little unsettled, her boyfriend told her to call the police. At that moment, a blast of icy air blew the door open and almost knocked the two to the ground. Completely unnerved, she went outside to wait. As soon as her boyfriend locked everything and started to leave, all the doors flew open and then slammed shut. When he walked around to secure everything again, all the doors were already locked.

Some people have supposedly photographed the Lady in Blue, and one woman reported an episode in the restroom. She, her sister, and her small son were walking by the bar one warm day and decided to stop in for a soda; during the daytime the bar provides an acceptable atmosphere for families. When they were finished, her sister went to the restroom while she and her son waited outside the door. When her sister came out, her son decided he needed to use the restroom also. Not wanting to send him into the men's room alone, she let him in to the ladies' room, knowing no one was there. A few minutes later her son came out almost in tears.

"What's wrong, sweetheart? What happened?"

He replied, "There's a blue lady in there. She told me to get out."

Angry and confused, the woman rushed into the restroom. It was empty.

For color and Key West atmosphere, Captain Tony's Saloon is a great place to pass the heat of the day or an evening. The entertainment is great, the beer is cold, patrons are friendly—and maybe you'll get to meet the Lady in Blue.

CHAPTER 4

Audubon House & Tropical Gardens
KEY WEST

I WAS STANDING ON THE SIDEWALK with a group of people, talking to Jon Engel, our ghost tour guide from The Original Key West Ghost Tours, when there was a commotion on the far side of the group.

"Look! Look!" someone called out.

We all turned to see what the person was so excited about. The man and his two companions were pointing at a third-story window.

"What are you pointing at?" everyone began to ask.

Breathless, he said, "There was a small face in that upstairs window. It was looking down at us, and then it just disappeared.

We all saw it." The other two nodded in agreement. They'd seen it, too.

Jon smiled. He hadn't even started talking about the Audubon House where we stood, and already things were happening. Sometimes on the tours people saw curtains moving, which might well have been caused by the air conditioning, or an occasional light switching on and off, if anything. But this was great. It was fun for him to watch people's reactions, and it was good for business. He knew Brant, his boss, would be pleased to hear about this experience.

After the excitement died down, Jon began his talk.

"Looks like the ghosts are trying to preempt me this evening," he laughed, "but, ghosts aside, this house—the Audubon House—has a fascinating history."

The house had been built by Captain John H. Geiger, a prosperous harbormaster and wrecker, one of those daring men who braved pirates and sometimes stormy seas to rescue passengers and salvage cargo from scuttled shipwrecks. Some think it was built in 1830, because in 1832 John James Audubon visited the Florida Keys and the Dry Tortugas aboard the Revenue Cutter, *Marion*. He allegedly sighted and drew eighteen new species of birds, many in the one-acre garden of the house, while he resided there as a guest. Research of tax rolls, deeds, and old newspaper articles, however, strongly suggests that he did not. His writings reflect that he stayed aboard the *Marion* to avoid the "fevers," as he had promised his wife. Also, he never mentioned the Geigers or the house in any of his writings. Also, the style of the house is American Classic Revival, and it was almost certainly built after the disastrous hurricane of 1846, probably about 1850, but not in 1830.

In 1829 Captain Geiger married Lucretia Sanders, a woman from the Bahamas, who bore him twelve children. Captain Geiger and his wife both died in the house, as well as five of their

children, one falling from a tree in the garden. Geiger descen-
dents lived there until 1956, the last being Willy Smith.

After Mr. Smith died, the house sat empty for two years. It
was saved from demolition by Colonel and Mrs. Mitchell Wolfson, who purchased it in 1958, renovated it, and opened it as a
museum in 1960. The house was Key West's first restoration
project and is still considered the crown jewel of all of the island's
restoration efforts. The house has been furnished with twenty-
eight first-edition Audubon paintings and with furniture typical
of the prosperous elegance of nineteenth-century Key West. The
garden, too, was restored to historic authenticity. It is now run by
the Mitchell Wolfson Family Foundation as a nonprofit, educational institution, which provides tours of the house and garden
and conducts art classes.

And there are the ghosts. I talked to Robert Merritt, the oper-
ations manager, who gave me much more of the history of the
house. He admitted that from time to time inexplicable things
happen. Light bulbs are unscrewed. The rocking chairs on the
porch rock back and forth on their own.

He told me that recently, while he was closing up one evening, he found beads from one of the several festivals on the
island scattered around the living room floor. He surmised that
some child had broken the string and just left the beads strewn
around the room. He picked them all up, threw them in the
trash, and finished locking up. He never gave the beads another
thought. When he returned the next morning, he discovered the
beads again scattered about the living room floor.

Visitors sometimes hear children laughing on the third floor
or whispering to each other. And, of course, there is the occasional face in the window that I almost saw. In fact, the third
floor might well be heavily haunted.

During the 1800s, yellow fever epidemics regularly swept
across the Keys, one of the reasons Audubon's wife didn't want

him to stay ashore when he visited in 1832. When you contract yellow fever, time is the only cure. If you catch the virus, which is transmitted by mosquitoes, your body either destroys the virus or you die. And yellow fever is very contagious. So when one of the Geiger children got sick, Mrs. Geiger isolated the child on the third floor of the house. Several of her children were infected with yellow fever; four of them died.

Willy Smith, the last Geiger descendent to live in the house, was an eccentric recluse, so the story goes. No one knows for sure when his peculiar behavior began, but in adulthood he never left the house. He seemed to spend most of his time on the second floor, where passersby would often see him looking out the window. The water and electricity in the house had been turned off, so he would lower a basket from a second floor window, and people would put food and water in it. Then he would hoist the basket back up. That was his only communication with the outside world.

Many years later, after the house had been restored and had become a museum, a wedding party reserved the house for a reception. The staff gave them a tour of the house. The whole house had been elegantly lighted with soft lamps and candles. When a group of guests went into what had been Willy's room on the second floor, the flames from the two candles burning there began to dance around the room, much to the fascination of the visitors. When the flames finally stopped moving, still separated from their candles, they formed a cross.

Willy was probably not the cleanest person. Occasionally, when a docent takes a party upstairs and into Willy's room, a strong scent of urine pervades the area. Fortunately, the docent will simply say in a stern voice, "Willy, get out of here and don't bother us," and the smell dissipates instantly. Willy appears to be as reclusive in death as he was in life.

But perhaps the most bizarre story concerning the Audubon

House is about the doll, variously called Mrs. Peck, Bye-Lo Baby, and the Demon Doll. Lore has it that the doll was made in England in the middle-to-late 1800s. The fashion at the time was to use a painting or oil-o-gram of a person, often a baby or young child, and create a doll in its exact likeness. This was especially popular when a young child had died.

When this particular doll was completed, it was placed next to the dead infant from whom it was copied, and no one could tell the difference between the two. Some speculate that the spirit of the deceased infant entered the doll. Others think that perhaps the spirit of one of the dead Geiger children possessed it. No one knows how the doll came into the Geigers' possession. In any case, someone in the Geiger family put the doll in a baby carriage in the third floor quarantine room, and many people insisted that its eyes followed them as they walked around.

Apparently, the doll did not like to be photographed. At one point, after the house had become a museum, its security system experienced a rash of what was thought to be false alarms. Each time the police and the museum director responded, but each time nothing had been taken, and there was no evidence of forced entry. Still, as a precaution, Bonnie Redmond prepared a photographic inventory of all the dozens and dozens of items in the house. When she got the photos back, she was stunned. All of the pictures of the doll had thick, black marks across their faces, as if Mrs. Peck were saying, "No pictures."

A few years later a BBC reporter working on a documentary of Key West came to the house. He took numerous pictures and interviewed several staff members about the history of the house and all the antiques, and he asked if there was anything unusual about the place. When the staff told him that they had a haunted doll, he laughed.

"You Americans, always making jokes."

At the end of the day, the Brit left the house, threw his camera and notebook in the passenger seat, and drove off. A half-block down Whitehead Street, his camera case popped open, the film fairly jumped out of the camera, and the roll of pictures he had just taken of the doll unraveled, destroying all the exposures. Needless to say, he was unnerved. He returned reluctantly the next day to reshoot the pictures he'd lost, but the doll was gone. Did a disgruntled docent remove her, or did she decide on her own that she was tired of being photographed? No one has ever figured out where she went, and there has never been any evidence to indicate what might have happened to her. The *Weekly World News* offered a five-thousand-dollar reward for the doll, dubbing her the "Demon Doll," but she is still out there roaming somewhere, the reward never having been claimed.

Even though the doll has left the premises, Willy Smith and the Geigers have not. The house continues to be very active. When Bob Merritt talks about the Audubon House he stresses the history and opulent décor—but he does admit it is haunted.

Spotlight on Chokoloskee

Nestled deep in the Everglades among the Ten Thousand Islands along the southwestern Gulf coast of Florida is the tiny village of Chokoloskee. It is at the end of the road—literally. You can't get any farther south except by boat. And at the end of the one main road in Chokoloskee is the Smallwood General Store, sitting on stilts, the waters of the Gulf lapping against its pilings as they have for over a hundred years. It was here on the shore next to Smallwood's that Ed Watson met his demise in 1910.

Ed Watson had come to the area several years before and was farming very successfully on forty acres a few miles south on the Chatham River. He was a quiet, angry man who kept to himself, but was often in trouble with the law because of his violent temper. He had many enemies in the neighborhood.

Because he was so standoffish, he was cloaked in mystery. No one knew much about him. Folks wondered how he was able to do so well with his farm in such a hostile environment, until disemboweled bodies began showing up in the waters around Watson's farm. Someone finally figured out that he had been hiring migrant workers and then killing them instead of paying them, disposing of their bodies by burying them on his farm or feeding them to the alligators.

The local sheriff formed a posse and proceeded to Watson's place to arrest him. Watson wasn't home, but the posse found a mass grave with dozen of bodies and body parts. Back at Smallwood's, the posse waited for Watson to show up. Because of the gruesomeness of the apparent murders, they dispensed with normal legal proceedings and shot him dead as soon as he appeared.

Many of the locals think Smallwood's is haunted by Ed Watson and that it's not safe to go among the pilings under the store. Maybe that's true, but there is no doubt that Watson's old place is filled with the ghosts of his murder victims. Many people have tried to make a go of the farm, but very little ever grew there after Watson died, and everyone has been overwhelmed by the ghosts. After many years, an old woman moved into Watson's house. She, too, encountered the phantoms, and one night, while trying to fend them off with a lighted knot torch, burned the place to the ground. Since then, snakes and vegetation have reclaimed the farm and the house.

Ed Watson may or may not be around, but the ghosts of his many victims still certainly occupy that forty acres on the Chatham River a few miles south of the Smallwood General Store in Chokoloskee.

CHAPTER 5

Marrero's Guest Mansion
KEY WEST

SARAH MARTIN* PICKED UP HER CLOTHES from the bed and turned to hang them in the armoire against the wall. She stepped forward and reached out to open the armoire when a woman floated out of it—right through the doors. Sarah screamed, dropped her clothes, and almost fainted. Moments later Sarah and her husband, Robert, were downstairs confronting James Remes, the owner of Marrero's Guest Mansion and innkeeper at the time, and asking to check out.

"We saw a ghost," Sarah said, still shaking. "She walked right out of the armoire, and the doors were still closed. Then she just vanished."

James tried to give the Martins a sympathetic smile.

"Yes, I know," he said. "The ghost you saw was Hetty Marrero, the wife of the man who built this house. Come on in to the parlor and have a glass of wine. I'll tell you the history of this place and its ghosts. Maybe I can convince you to stay; I'll even put you in another room, if you wish."

The Martins followed James into the parlor.

Francisco Marrero was a Cuban and had been thrown into prison during a revolution in the 1870s. He wasn't there long. He bribed his way out and fled to Europe. While he was in Spain, he met and fell in love with Enriquetta Gonzales Ruiz, a striking Andalusian beauty from Seville. Still on the run from Cuban authorities and with limited resources, Marrero was unable to convince her to marry him. Dejected, he left for New York, where he learned the cigar-making business and then moved to Key West to start his own cigar factory.

Within a few years he was a wealthy man with six hundred employees and a business worth half-a-million dollars. Enriquetta, "Hetty," was still on his mind, so he built what became known as the Marrero Mansion on Fleming Street, then left for Spain in hopes of winning her hand. A few months later he returned to Key West with his bride and took up residence in the mansion.

As far as anyone knows, Hetty and Francisco were happy in their life together in Key West. She had a beautiful house with plenty of money coming in from the cigar factory, and she bore Francisco eight children. But all was not to end well.

From time to time, Francisco went to Cuba on tobacco-buying trips; he was no longer persona non grata. On one such trip he died. His death certificate stated that he had died under mysterious circumstances. Hetty was devastated by the news, as anyone can well imagine, but she was consoled by the fact that she had a grand home and a healthy income. And, of course, she had her eight children to comfort her.

A few weeks after the funeral, however, one Señora Maria Ignacia Garcia de Marrero arrived in Key West by ship with her husband's last will and testament. She was Francisco's first wife, whom he had neglected to divorce, a nearly impossible task in Catholic Cuba, before he married Hetty. A bitter legal battle ensued, and Hetty lost. She lost everything—the cigar factory, her only source of income, and, most devastatingly, her house. She and her eight children were summarily thrown out into the streets.

As she was being evicted by the sheriff, she stood on the steps, looked at the mansion one last time and said to passersby and anyone who would listen, "Here today you are witnessing a grave injustice. Although you remove me now from this house, you should know that it is rightfully mine, and here I shall remain even if only in spirit."

Key West in those days was a pretty rough town. Within two years Hetty and all her children were dead. Her oldest son committed suicide. She and the rest of her family died in the streets of Key West from consumption, diphtheria, and yellow fever.

Maria Garcia de Marrero sold the cigar factory and the house, liquidating all of her husband's assets and returning to Cuba a very wealthy woman. Later, however, she was implicated in Francisco Marrero's untimely and mysterious death.

Enriquetta meant it when she said that she would remain in the house forever. So far, she has. James Remes and his guests have had many exciting experiences in the mansion. When he bought it in 1983, it had been a residence, a law office, a bordello, and a restaurant and casino. James turned it into a bed-and-breakfast.

The Martins, who did remain but moved to another room, were not the first guests to see Hetty walk out of the armoire in Room 18. The adjacent room had been a nursery, and there was a long-sealed door behind the armoire. To Hetty, of course, it didn't matter. She still went in and out of the nursery checking on her children. She also wandered throughout the rest of the house, as she does to this day.

The mansion's heavy, wooden front door shakes, windows rattle, lamps switch off and on, and a light often flashes in the attic. Guests have seen Hetty walking down the hall and up and down the stairs. Many times guests sitting in the living room will see a shadow descending the stairs and expect to see a person following. They are surprised to see just the shadow continue on down the stairs, across the hall, and out through the front door, which remains closed. At other times guests will see a woman standing in the hall, and when they address her, she vanishes.

A crystal chandelier, a stunning antique piece, lights the front hallway. Hetty is a welcoming person, but occasionally someone with negative energy will come into the house. The chandelier will begin to rattle and sway, and the person will inexplicably get tense and nervous. Most often they just leave without checking in. Those who do stay usually have bad experiences and decide to check out.

Jeffery Beane* and a friend checked in one weekend and were staying in Room 18. The first morning they were there, Jeffery awoke to see a woman standing at the foot of the bed looking in the mirror and brushing her hair. Shocked, he reached over to wake up his friend.

The woman turned and stared at him, put her finger to her lips and whispered, "Don't wake your friend."

Startled, he grabbed his friend's arm and started to sit up. Hetty was immediately at his side and covered his mouth with her hand. He jerked back and flew out of bed, and Hetty evaporated instantly.

John Diebold is the current owner and ran the place himself for many years. Steve and Jackie Mackiewcz visited every year for ten years until John finally lured them to Key West permanently to be the innkeepers.

Sue and I visited the bed-and-breakfast on a warm September afternoon. We sat on the porch with Steve in comfortable wicker chairs enjoying a cool breeze and watching the tourists pass by. Steve related some of his and Jackie's experiences in the mansion. On their first night as innkeepers Jackie saw Hetty walk right through a wall. Not long after, Jackie's laptop with a fingerprint and retina security system booted up all by itself. Recently, Steve and Jackie were enjoying a quiet evening together, sitting on a couch reading. Jackie got up to go to the kitchen for a cup of coffee. Steve looked in her direction and was surprised to see her shadow moving in the opposite direction. As she rose, her shadow was actually sitting down. Moments later, after Jackie returned and sat down again, the TV came on—to a porn station!

And then there are the keys. Steve's and Jackie's keys continually disappear and eventually reappear in odd places. The week before our visit, Steve went to retrieve his car keys to run an errand. They were gone from the peg in the kitchen where he normally keeps them. Two days later, one of the staff found them on the front steps.

In spite of the sometimes startling experiences that staff and guests have had at Marrero's, most seem to enjoy having Hetty around. It's all in good fun, and very few get upset from their experiences with her.

As one guest put it, "It's almost like visiting my grandmother's house. It seems that Hetty gives the mansion a homey, lived-in feel. I like having her around. If nothing else, she's a great topic of conversation."

Spotlight on The Everglades

Everglades National Park is a vast, million-and-a-half acre wilderness, which covers most of south Florida. It's ironic that the state's most populated area lies just to the east of its most isolated.

On the evening of December 29, 1972, Eastern Flight 401, a Lockheed L1011 Tri-Star, was flying into Miami International Airport. Captain Robert Loft and Second Officer Don Repo began their approach and were lowering the landing gear when the captain noticed that the nose gear light and some of the other landing gear lights were not illuminated. That indicated that the nose and other landing gear were not down and locked in position. Captain Loft so informed the control tower, which directed him to circle the airport at an altitude of two thousand feet.

Although the altimeter and auto-pilot indicators were both lit, the crew realized too late that the plane was rapidly descending. The last, chilling words from the flight recorder were the captain's: "What? We're at two thousand feet, right . . . Hey, what's happening here? Tower . . . Impact!" Then Flight 401 disappeared. The plane had crashed into Shark River Slough in the Everglades. Ninety-eight of the 163 people aboard, including the entire crew, perished.

Shortly after the accident, an Eastern Airline executive was flying to Miami on another Tri-Star similar to the Flight 401 plane. He sat in first class next to an Eastern Airline pilot in uniform, and assumed the man was headed home. Not unusual. But the pilot sat staring out the window, even when the executive tried to converse with him. Finally, the pilot turned to face him, and, aghast, the executive recognized the face of Captain Robert Loft. Instantly, the ghost evaporated.

Immediately after the crash, cleanup crews went into the Everglades to search for human remains and remove wreckage.

The crews worked late into the night under the strong glare of large search lights, and would often hear screams, moans, and whimpering coming from the slough. Very unnerving.

One evening, a crew member in a johnboat heard moans coming from an area thick with saw grass. He guided his boat to the spot where he thought the sounds were coming from. As he plowed into the grass, he was horrified to see in the dark, tannin-stained waters the eyeless, bleached-white face of a man, his mouth open as if screaming. The crewman quickly poled his boat back out of the grass and screamed to his companions, "I found a body! I found a body!" When the others rushed to his aid, they saw nothing. There was no body.

Over the years since the crash, many have seen both Captain Loft and Second Officer Don Repo on flights to south Florida. And even to this day, airboat captains who run tours to the site hear moans and see ghastly faces in the dark waters of these haunted swamps in the Everglades.

CHAPTER 6

Historic Biltmore Hotel of Coral Gables
MIAMI

MIAMI WAS A NICE CHANGE after our time in the Keys, still leisurely but a little more exciting. Miami proper has a population of less than four hundred thousand, but Miami-Dade County has over two million people, and it's difficult to know which city you're in as you drive from Homestead to West Palm Beach. The area has a colorful history, which goes back only to the late 1800s, when Henry Flagler tired of St. Augustine and set his sights on the southeast coast.

In the early 1900s George Merrick, a land developer, created Coral Gables, just west of Miami, as a suburb intended for affluent residents. He built wide, tree-lined boulevards, huge Mediterranean-style mansions, lush golf courses, and country clubs, landscaped with banyan trees and tropical foliage.

In 1925 he teamed with hotel magnate John Bowman to begin construction on a "great hotel . . . which would not only serve as a hostelry to the crowds thronging to Coral Gables, but also would serve as a center of sports and fashion."

Ten months and ten million dollars later, the Biltmore opened, with its spectacular tower patterned after the Giralda in Seville, Spain, a huge swimming pool for aquatic events, two eighteen-hole golf courses, canals with gondolas, a polo grounds, and cavernous ballrooms among its many amenities.

During the "Roaring Twenties" and later the Depression, the Biltmore was alive with activity and events that drew thousands. In the depths of the Depression, the hotel stayed alive with synchronized swimming demonstrations, a four-year-old phenomenon who dove from an eighty-five-foot platform, and alligator wrestling.

In 1942 as World War II developed into a global conflict, the War Department converted the Biltmore into the Army Air Force Regional Hospital, which treated wounded soldiers and aviators returning from overseas. Windows were sealed with concrete for the blackout. Marble floors were covered with utilitarian linoleum. Rooms were converted to sick wards, operating rooms, and administrative offices. There was even a morgue constructed on a lower floor.

The University of Miami School of Medicine was housed in the building for a time, and after the war, the hotel remained as a Veteran's Administration Hospital until 1968.

The building sat empty for five years until the City of Coral Gables, through the Historic Monuments Act and Legacy of Parks program, took possession. It remained empty for another ten years while the City decided what to do with it. Finally, in 1983, Coral Gables began restoring the old hostelry, and after four years and fifty-five-million dollars, it opened again as a grand hotel. It remained open only three years because of the poor economy in the late 1980s and once again sat empty.

But in June 1992, the Seaways Hotels Corporation bought the building and began a ten-year, forty-million-dollar renovation with a remarkable team of architects and engineers, including the acclaimed interior designer, Lynn Wilson. Guest rooms were renovated, new computer and telephone systems were installed, and the seven-hundred-thousand-gallon swimming pool was resurfaced with polished marble. The Biltmore is once again the crown jewel of Coral Gables.

Joanne, my ghost-magnet pal, hadn't been able to go to the Keys with Sue and me, but she joined us now on our Miami visit. Our first stop was the Biltmore.

Sue was amazed at the changes. During summers when she was in high school, she had visited a friend who had moved to Coral Gables. On one visit, the girls went to the VA hospital, where her friend's father worked, and they were able to tour the facility, even going to the top of the tower for a view of the city. She remembered the hospital as a very austere place, very clean, but lacking any aesthetic value. The walls were painted in putrid government green. She was astounded by the renovation, the beautiful carpeting, the paintings, and furnishings. It definitely was not the same building she had been in so long ago.

Joanne, of course, was in her element. As she is prone to do, she struck up conversations with maintenance workers, maids, and even guests we met in the hallways, and we heard dozens of stories. She also discovered several entities roaming the halls just as we were, especially in the area that had housed the morgue. One of the maintenance workers whom we spoke with told us that even to this day, lights are turned on and off, and music with no identifiable source is heard. He said that once as he was standing in the lobby late in the evening, he heard a loud crash, which sounded like a large vase or urn being smashed to the floor. When he looked around, everything was in order.

A maid told us that a young woman wearing a white dress had died in the Biltmore in a fall from a fifth-floor balcony. Her six-year-old son had been playing on the balcony and had climbed onto the railing just as she had entered the room. Horrified, she rushed to grab him off the railing and fell over herself. Now a residual haunting, she is seen in various rooms and hallways by many of the guests. Joanne was thrilled later to see the woman in the hallway.

The "Woman in White," as she is called, is well known at the Biltmore, but the most famous—or infamous—ghost is that of Fatty Walsh, Miami's most powerful gangster during Prohibition years. Among his many illegal enterprises, Fatty ran a speakeasy and casino on the thirteenth floor of the hotel. He was known by everyone who was anyone in Miami. Gangsters, movie stars, sports figures, and politicians, even the police, knew Fatty Walsh. He had hundreds of friends, but he also had a good share of enemies. As the story goes, one night an angry patron who'd lost a fortune, or perhaps a hit man for another crime boss, shot him in the crowded casino.

With Fatty Walsh gone, the hotel closed and cleaned the casino, but Fatty's legend—and maybe his ghost—has lived on. He chain-smoked cigars, enjoyed good liquor, and liked his women. Even to this day, people report smelling cigar smoke in the halls, and women especially experience strange sensations as they move around the hotel.

In one especially bizarre incident, a young couple was exploring the hotel and stepped into an elevator. Before they had a chance to push any buttons, the door closed, and the elevator rose, stopping at the thirteenth floor. That floor is now a private suite and accessible only with a specially coded key, but the door opened. The couple stood in the elevator for a moment, then the very attractive young woman stepped out into the suite. The door shut rapidly, and the elevator started down. The woman's husband, beside himself, began pushing buttons but to no avail until the elevator stopped in the lobby, and the door opened again.

Frantic, the young man raced off the elevator to find a bellhop. Although he was reluctant to believe the man because he knew that suite was unoccupied at the time, the bellhop used his coded key to take them back up to the thirteenth-floor suite. When the elevator door opened, the young woman rushed into her husband's arms. She related to the men that as she had stood in the suite, she had been enveloped by cold air and could smell a very strong scent of cigar smoke, although she couldn't see any. She also had heard music and people talking and laughing. She'd had the overwhelming sense that someone was standing right behind her and had even called out to see if anyone were there, but no one answered.

Finally, there is the story of a certain politician in the 1990s who was staying in the thirteenth-floor suite and wanted to watch a Saturday afternoon football game. When he turned on the television, there was nothing but snow and static. His Secret Service men quickly called the hotel engineer, who could find nothing wrong with the TV set. Even when sets were switched, there was no reception. The politician eventually had to leave the hotel to view the game at a friend's house. Perhaps Fatty Walsh was a Republican.

Joanne, Sue, and I spent the entire afternoon meandering around the place. It seemed to be a slow day, and the employees and guests we met were willing to stop and chat, regaling us with stories of the strange things that had happened in the hotel.

The Biltmore Hotel may or may not be the most haunted hotel in America, but it is certainly one of the most luxurious. If Fatty Walsh truly does haunt its halls, he has chosen a wonderful place to spend eternity.

Spotlight on Miami River Inn

Miami River Inn is a cozy little jewel nestled on the Miami Canal just south of I-395 and west of I-95. And it is a real hideaway, nothing fancy but very comfortable, close to downtown Miami, the beach, and dozens of great restaurants. In former times, it was the destination of presidents, celebrities, and dignitaries. Henry Flagler even stayed at the hotel in the early 1900s. It is not only a hostelry of note, it is also haunted. The inn was built in 1910 and has seen several makeovers. Reportedly, it was once a funeral parlor. Maybe that's why it's haunted. Or maybe not.

In one of the rooms (let's call it room 12), there seems to be a residual haunting that replays itself every day at 11 P.M., very inconvenient if you're not a night owl. First, precisely at eleven, a door opens and slams shut, very loudly. Then what sounds like feet being wiped on a doormat can be heard. Next there is silence, followed by the sound of running feet—and it sounds like it's coming right into room 12. Then the door of the room rattles, and the knob actually shakes, followed by crashing lamps, vases, pictures. In room 12, it sounds as if someone is ransacking the room above. Then more running feet, bounding up the stairs, followed by the sound of the door of the room above room 12 opening and slamming shut again. After a moment of silence, the furniture upstairs begins to move around, scraping, bumping, thumping, smashing against the walls and the floor. The vibrations can be felt in room 12. After an hour, it finally stops. Now, if you can, you're free to go to sleep. Nothing will happen again until 11 P.M. tomorrow. If you're a morning person and like to go to bed early, perhaps you shouldn't stay in this room. On the other hand, if you're not there for the nightlife, why are you in Miami?

CHAPTER 7

The Colony Hotel & Cabaña Club

DELRAY BEACH

THE COLONY HOTEL AND CABAÑA CLUB is not the Biltmore, but it is a really spectacular hotel. The three of us—Joanne, Sue, and I—had spent most of the previous day and evening exploring the Biltmore and talking to people there. We were tired, but the following morning we got an early start and drove the fifty miles north to Delray Beach, just above Boca Raton.

Delray Beach, with a population of only sixty thousand, is on the fringe of the greater Miami metropolitan area and is slower paced and less frenetic than Miami. One of only two hundred hotels nationwide that are members of The National Trust for Historic Preservation, the Colony Hotel fits right in with the more casual and old-Florida ambiance of the town.

Like the Biltmore, the Colony, sister hotel to the Colony in Kennebunkport, Maine, was built in 1926 by father and son, Charles and George Bowden, to cater to the hordes of well-to-do Northerners who flocked to Florida during the 1920s to escape the cold, snowy winters and bask in the sunshine and leisurely Florida lifestyle.

Remodeled several years ago, the architecture retains its 1920s character with pine floors, a wood-burning marble-and-coral fireplace in the lobby, ceiling fans, wood shutters, and rattan furniture. At the same time, it is one of the most environmentally progressive hotels in the country. Aerosol spray products and toxic cleaning materials have been eliminated from the seventy guest rooms. The management recycles wherever possible in guest rooms and administrative spaces and uses biodegradable and recycled products throughout. Dozens of live plants keep the air fresh and natural in interior areas.

For many years the hotel was closed during summer months, when the entire staff moved to its sister hotel in Kennebunkport. Furniture was covered with sheets. All but a few lights and all other nonessential electricity were turned off. Cobwebs and dust collected in corners, windowsills, furniture, and floors. A caretaker was left behind to perform minimal maintenance on the grounds, cutting grass, watering plants, and providing some security. But in summer, even with a caretaker around, the Colony looked mostly abandoned, forlorn, and even ghostly.

Perhaps because the hotel was closed much of the year and for so many years, rumors of strange happenings grew about the place, tales of mysterious lights, sightings of apparitions, unexplained sounds emanating from the building. Maybe they were true or maybe they were just the imaginings of strollers passing by in the dark. In any case, the Colony developed a reputation for being haunted.

One summer evening during the off-season, a couple was walking down the street past the empty hotel and saw, or thought they saw, movement inside. The figures they saw seemed to be running back and forth in the darkened building. They thought perhaps kids had broken into the place and were robbing or ransacking it. This was in the days before cell phones, so they crossed the street to a gas station and called the police, who quickly responded.

Several squad cars arrived, and officers walked around the exterior to check for signs of a break-in. There were none, so they contacted the caretaker to get permission to enter. Inside, a quick check revealed that all the doors were locked and the alarm system was functioning properly. It had not been tampered with. One officer was standing in the lobby when suddenly the elevator started rumbling as if it were moving. Then it stopped and chimed, the usual signal indicating that it had arrived at the desired floor. The doors opened, but no one came out. The officer stood there watching, dumbstruck. Now quite nervous, he radioed his partner, who joined him in the lobby. Together they finished their investigation and left, the caretaker locking up and resetting the alarm behind them. They had found nothing out of order.

During the same period passersby began reporting orbs, or balls of light, flying erratically in front of second-story windows. These orbs became quite common for several months, and many people reported seeing them. Then, as suddenly as they had begun appearing, they disappeared. None have been reported since 1989.

In 1999 the hotel began staying open year-round, and the stories of paranormal activity have persisted. Guests have reported strange lights and dark figures moving through the hotel, and some have heard music coming from the darkened and empty dining room. The music can be heard only on moonless nights and early in the morning, before 3 A.M. And some have heard female voices coming from the dining room, when no one was there.

One staff member reported that on several occasions he has heard noises from the empty kitchen: pots clanging, utensils being dropped, an occasional plate shattering on the floor. He said that, each time, he went in to see what was going on, half expecting to find a mess. What he found was a kitchen in perfect order, pots hanging and dishes stacked where they should be.

Justina Broughton, Charles Bowden's granddaughter, has reported hearing animated discussions coming from the office and the kitchen. When she was a child during the off-season, she would often accompany her father into the closed hotel and run through the halls and empty rooms. She recalls that she often caught fleeting glimpses of something or someone out of the corner of her eye and thought nothing of it at the time. And more than once she saw an older, well-dressed man reflected in the glass cover of a painting. She had the odd sensation that he was her grandfather, and well he may have been. In any case, her experiences were always benign, even pleasant.

We were welcomed by a friendly staff. Although most of the people we talked to were a bit reluctant to discuss the paranormal activity there, they allowed us to roam around and take a look for ourselves.

As we walked around, Joanne was able to confirm many of the stories we had heard from others or read about. She saw dark, fleeting figures in the dining room and hallways and heard the clanging of pots and pans coming from the kitchen, as well as music and muffled voices in the dining room. She didn't find anything peculiar about the elevator but did sense activity on the second floor. Mostly, she confirmed what we already knew.

We couldn't stay very late, so we were not able to experience any-thing that might be taking place in the wee hours, but I have no doubt of their veracity.

As we left the Colony, I promised Sue I'd bring her back for a long weekend. It seemed a wonderful, romantic place for a getaway.

CHAPTER 8

Riddle House
West Palm Beach

WHEN WE THINK OF PIONEERS, many of us automatically picture Conestoga wagons crossing the prairie, sod huts, settlers fighting off Indian attacks from encircled wagons. As for me, I like to think of the pioneers who settled Florida during the same time that others were conquering the West. Crackers endured just as many hardships as their Western counterparts, braving the thick, often impassable palmetto scrub and swamps, as well as the intense heat, snakes, Indians, and outlaws preying on them. Today, fortunately, tiny pockets of the early history of Florida have been preserved around the state.

One such is Yesteryear Village, a ten-acre plot in the South Florida Fairgrounds in West Palm Beach, which has on display a variety of original and reproduction structures from the mid-1800s to the mid-1900s. There is a "shotgun" house, a general store, a school, a blacksmith's shop, a farmhouse, and a 1960s gas station. Villagers in period costumes wander through the complex, cooking in old-fashioned kitchens with wood-burning stoves, making horseshoes and implements in the blacksmith shop, repairing shoes, carrying on the activities typical of a small community from the past.

Nestled among the various buildings is the Riddle House, an intriguing place—and very haunted. This was the last stop on our swing through South Florida. Joanne was excited. The Riddle House had been her dormitory when she attended Palm Beach Atlantic College, now Palm Beach Atlantic University.

The house was built in 1904 as a funeral home on property next to the old Woodlawn Cemetery on Acacia Road. Being adjacent to the cemetery was convenient for the undertaker, who also provided at least some security. The graveyard at that time was considered a high-crime area, because so many bodies were exhumed for the possessions buried with them. The house was known then as the Gatekeeper's Cottage.

During those early years, a local resident murdered one of the cemetery workers, a man named Buck, after a violent argument. Almost immediately, there were reports of an apparition, presumed to be Buck, walking around the cemetery and the cottage. This apparition seemed to be residual. Buck was simply going about his job, apparently not aware that he was dead.

In 1920 West Palm Beach hired a city manager, Karl Riddle, and, to cut costs, moved him and his family into the cottage. It soon became known as the Riddle House. The Riddles enjoyed living there. Buck was not much in evidence and was not threatening when he was seen.

Toward the end of the Great Depression in the late 1930s, one of Riddle's employees, despondent and depressed over his financial situation and the turmoil it had created in his family, went up to the attic of the house and hanged himself. Riddle was devastated by the incident and fell into a deep depression himself.

The beam from which the man had committed suicide was immediately replaced, but soon after the death, workers, visitors, and the Riddles themselves began seeing shadows and dark figures out of the corners of their eyes. People reported hearing muffled conversations and strange noises. Many heard footsteps on the stairs and the upper floors, including the attic. It was not long before workers refused to enter the house and even quit. Eventually, Karl Riddle and his family moved out.

For many years, various businesses occupied the house. They all failed. The building again became the cemetery sexton's home for a short time. Eventually, Palm Beach Atlantic College took over the building and made it a women's dormitory, housing six female students.

In 1980, the city condemned the house because it was in disrepair. John Riddle, Karl's nephew, asked the city for the building because of its historical value. He determined to rescue it, and moved it to its present location in Yesteryear Village at the Fairgrounds, where it was restored.

The restoration was shrouded with many strange and inexplicable occurrences. Tools locked up in the living room at the end of a day's work would be found the next morning in an upstairs bedroom. Wood neatly stacked in the dining room would be piled humble-jumble outside. Attic windows would be shattered three or four nights in a row, glass both inside and outside the house and no projectile to indicate how the windows had been broken.

Several incidents occurred in the attic. One carpenter was hit by a flying piece of wood. A paint can lid flew across the room and hit another worker in the head. One morning paint cans were found opened, paint poured all over the attic floor. Finally, workers stopped going to the attic entirely.

Many heard footsteps and muffled voices from empty rooms, even chains being dragged down the stairs. Another worker was hit by a piece of flying wood on the stairway. It wasn't long before workers became rattled and frightened; many quit. The project ground to a halt and was discontinued for several months.

Work finally resumed, and the restoration was completed. A grand opening was planned, and the newly renovated Riddle House was opened to the public. During the celebration, a couple dressed in period clothes wandered from room to room. Everyone thought they were there to provide color and lend atmosphere to the festivities. After the celebration ended, however, someone realized that the couple strolling around was the same couple pictured in an old 1920s photograph hanging on the living room wall. Even more bizarre, when the newspaper photographer sorted through his pictures of the event, the couple was nowhere to be seen.

Joanne resided in the Riddle House from 1978 to 1980. She never heard any chains being dragged down the stairs or muffled voices from empty rooms, but she did often see a man walking down the staircase. Joanne is and has always been a night owl, so she does her best work in the evening. On many nights, as she sat up tap-tap-tapping on her portable typewriter in the living room surrounded by quarts of Howard Johnson's pistachio ice cream, she would look up to see a man on the stairs watching her. Because she had grown up in a haunted house and was so sensitive herself, she thought nothing of it. Sometimes she'd hear footsteps on the stairs and, worried that she was disturbing her housemates, would go into the hall to see who was there. The only person she ever saw was the apparition. She didn't know where he went when he disappeared or if he went back to the attic, because she knew nothing of the attic. When she lived there, the attic door was locked, and the girls were told it was a janitor's closet. No one ever told her and the other girls about the man who had hanged himself there.

Joanne has never been particularly afraid of the paranormal, but there were occasions in the Riddle House when she was a bit unnerved. Two of her dorm mates lived in a very small room in the back of the place. There was no window and only enough space for one bunk bed, one desk, one chair, and one small dresser. It was more like a short hallway than a room, and two people could not walk around in the place at the same time.

When her friends were gone on weekends, Joanne liked to stay there, because she had more privacy and the use of a small television she could watch all night without being disturbed or bothering anyone else.

Unfortunately, the room always felt a bit creepy to her—and not just because it was so tiny and claustrophobic, or because of the toadstools that often grew out of the damp carpet. Joanne always felt she was being watched in that room. Not even her male apparition from the staircase came in. To ease her mind, she always kept a light and the TV on when she stayed there.

She and her roommate lived in the house alone for two months during the summer of 1980, attending summer school. She recalls that the three of them—she, her roommate, and their ghostie friend from the stairs—were perfectly content. The only place she ever felt uneasy was in that back room.

When Joanne, Sue, and I arrived, both the Fairgrounds and the Riddle House were packed with visitors. Joanne was a bit disappointed that she didn't have the opportunity to spend any time in the house alone, but she did enjoy wandering through it, reminiscing about her wild and crazy days as a college student. When we left, I promised her we'd come back down when it was quiet. Maybe she'd even have the chance to see her old ghostie friend on the staircase.

Spotlight on Coral Castle

In the late 1800s, Edward Leedskalnin left his Latvian home and came to North America. The love of his life, sixteen-year-old Hermine Lusis, had jilted him on the eve of their wedding because she had decided that, at twenty-six, he was too old for her and too weird. Brokenhearted and dejected, he turned his back on Latvia to build a new life across the Atlantic.

After several years of wandering across Canada and the United States, he contracted tuberculosis and came to Florida for his health, buying a small acreage in Florida City, a few miles south of Homestead.

There in 1923, he began building Rock Gate Park, using massive blocks of coral to fashion huge tables, chairs, couches, fountains, and pillars. Coral weighs 125 pounds per cubic foot and is difficult to work with. Leedskalnin was five feet tall and weighed one hundred pounds, and yet he was able to extract coral from the ground, carve it into a myriad of shapes—like a three-ton table in the shape of Florida—and move the objects around the grounds of the park. He worked at night in secrecy with no help, using the most fundamental of tools.

In 1937, with development threatening the peace and quiet of Rock Gate Park, he moved his creations north to a ten-acre plot of ground near Homestead. Neighbors saw him transporting his sculptures on a heavy trailer pulled by a borrowed tractor, but no one ever saw how he loaded them.

In this new location, Edward built what he called the Coral Castle, a two-story tower house using 235 tons of coral. The gate to his sanctuary was made of nine tons of coral, and was so perfectly balanced that it could be opened with one finger.

As he had earlier, he worked at night in secrecy, and no one ever saw how he managed to extract the gigantic blocks of coral from the ground, carve them, and lift them into position. Some believed he had supernatural help. Some thought he used witchcraft. The fact is that, even though he had only a fourth-grade education, he studied physics, astronomy, and geology throughout his life and was an outstanding engineer.

He died in 1951 from cancer, but some believe Edward stayed on at his beloved Coral Castle. Several psychics claim to have conversed with him, and many people feel the powerful energy that exudes from the place. One visitor took pictures, which, when developed, showed figures that were not there when he snapped the photos. Whether or not Coral Castle is haunted may still be open to question, but its construction will forever be shrouded in mystery.

CHAPTER 9

Arcadia's Old Opera House & Museum

ARCADIA

CHASING GHOSTS FOR *America's Haunted Road Trip* could sometimes be quite frustrating, especially in a state like Florida, which is about one thousand miles from one end to the other. There were people who had promised what sounded like a great story, but after I'd driven to the other end of the state, I'd meet someone who didn't have any evidence and only wanted publicity.

And then there were the no-shows. Driving three or four hours to meet a contact who doesn't appear can drive you crazy, and that's what happened to me in Punta Gorda. My contact, a tour operator, was supposed to meet Sue and me but never showed. Needless to say, I was miffed, but when one door closes, another often opens.

As we wandered around town, by chance we met Louie Desguin, a Punta Gorda native, river boat captain and tour guide, and passionate historian. When I told him what I was up to, he said, "You have to contact the Peace River Ghost Tracker team—great people and highly respected investigators. They'll help you out."

And that's how we found ourselves at the Opera House in nearby Arcadia with Scott Walker, Sprout Dvorak (she's only five feet tall), and some of the members of their PRGT team, Tom and Toni Land and their daughter, Geri. We all gathered on the street in front of the Opera House, then climbed the steep stairs to meet Paula Rhoads, owner of The Shops Upstairs within Arcadia's Old Opera House & Museum, and to talk about the history and hauntings of this colorful icon, one of 374 buildings in town listed on the National Registry of Historic Places.

On Thanksgiving Day, 1905, a fire roared through the business district. Some say it was started by a drunken cowboy who accidentally knocked over a lantern in the livery stables, but no one will ever know for sure. When the conflagration was finally extinguished, virtually all of downtown Arcadia lay in ashes.

Discouraged but not defeated, the townspeople quickly began to rebuild. First, the city council passed an ordinance decreeing that all buildings would henceforth be made of stone or brick. John J. Heard, the local banker and owner of the Florida Loan and Trust Company, immediately began building what became the DeSoto Opera House. The street floor housed his bank. Steep steps led up to the second story, which contained a large auditorium with a stage on the west end and a balcony on the east. It was used for movies, traveling shows, dances, political meetings, church and school events, and for a time as the USO.

A wide hallway ran along the south and east sides of the theater and separated it from offices on the south and east walls. Dressing rooms lined the north wall next to the stage. Heard rented the offices to local businessmen to help them get back on their feet. Local historian Howard Melton recalls that when he was a child, adults watched movies in the auditorium while the children played tag in the hallway or down on the street. After the adults had seen their show, the children were ushered in for their own movie. Today the old theater, dressing rooms, offices, and hallway are filled with antiques and museum pieces.

Paula had many stories of ghostly activity to tell. Often when there are few people in the store, she can go to one of the back rooms and hear what sounds like a large crowd in the theater area. When she returns to the auditorium, no one is there. Paula and many others hear children talking, laughing, and running around in the hallway, in front of the stage, and on the main staircase, as well as footsteps on the stage. And a local couple claim that long after the store had closed for the day, they saw a young girl in what they described as a party dress at a window in the corner room on the second floor.

A year before our visit, a woman was browsing around the store and wandered up to the stage. Paula happened to be looking in her direction when the woman got a confused look on her face, turned, and hurried down to Paula at the counter.

A bit flustered, she asked, "Is this place haunted?"

Paula smiled, "Actually, it is. Why do you ask?"

The woman sheepishly replied, "Well, I was just up on the stage and heard what sounded like quite a party up on the catwalk above the stage, but when I looked up, no one was there."

Trying not to laugh, Paula replied, "That could be. Weird things happen here."

Then a few months before Sue and I visited, the same woman was again browsing in a corner room when she saw a man who kept telling her "No!" "No!" in a very stern voice, as if he didn't want her there, then disappeared. The woman hurried down the hall to tell Paula what had happened and noticed a painting hanging on the wall. It was a portrait of the same man she'd just seen—John J. Heard, the banker who had built the Opera House in 1906.

Mr. Heard seems to be persnickety. A short time before this incident, Paula was sitting at the counter. No one was in the store. Suddenly, she heard a loud noise in the hall. Rushing out, she found a mask lying on the floor at the top of the stairs. The mask had been nailed to a music machine in front of Mr. Heard's portrait, nine feet away.

PRGT has investigated the Opera House several times. It's a great site to train new members how to use their array of cameras, DVMR systems, tape recorders, pyrometers, EMF meters, thermal cameras, compasses, and even dowsing rods.

During one of their investigations, Craig, Toni, and several members of the team were walking around the north end of the building when Toni entered one of the dressing rooms adjacent to the stage and began smelling fruity chewing gum. The others followed her in and smelled the gum also. Then the odor disappeared. When they left and entered the next dressing room, the same thing happened. The gum smell pervaded the room and then disappeared. The scent followed them from room to room for about fifteen minutes and then disappeared completely. But at the conclusion of their investigation, as they all assembled at the top of the main staircase, the odor once again enveloped them all for a few minutes and then dissipated.

While conducting a later investigation, Toni, Craig, and Scott were walking across the stage when they started smelling gum again. As in the earlier episode, the odor seemed to follow the team around and then disappear.

The team has always experienced activity at the north end of the building. Once when Toni was doing a temperature sweep, out of the corner of her eye she saw movement in a dressing room doorway. When she turned to look at it directly, a pulsating light rose out of the floor to knee height for about eight seconds, then vanished back into the floor.

PRGT has never encountered the "party" heard on the catwalk by The Shops Upstairs patron, but they have had their moments on the stage. Mike and Toni were in the center of the stage and observed a tall, shadowy person leaning against the wall near the steps down to the dressing rooms. When the "person" disappeared toward the dressing rooms, they raced after him. The dressing rooms were all empty.

On another occasion Vicki was sitting on stage, and when she stood up something tugged her hair. She quickly sat again, thinking her hair might have been caught on a nearby rope or other object. When she looked around, it was obvious that no obstructions were close enough, but when she stood again, something once more tugged her hair.

Later Thomas was standing in the hall doorway adjacent to the stage when he saw a huge, dark shadow of a person on the stage. The shadow was so large it blocked out all light coming in through a stage window. Moments later it dissolved.

Scott, Sprout, and their team have had just as many encounters at the other end of the building and in the rooms along the west side. In one of the back rooms, Scott sat in a chair making notes. Almost immediately he was overcome by a wave of nausea, and his chest was constricted. He jumped up as Lori entered the room.

"Lori, come sit in this chair." Lori sat down. Immediately, she too felt nauseous. Scott was thrilled.

"That's exactly what I felt!"

Moments later Toni came in, and Scott asked her to sit. Same reaction. But there was more. All at once Scott felt the presence of a German woman and heard, "Vas ist loss?"

"What does that mean, Toni?"

Toni answered, "It means 'What's wrong?'" then repeated in German "Vas ist loss?" Instantly, frigid air blasted her right side and a prickly sensation made her hair stand on end. As Toni jumped out of the chair, Scott smiled.

"I guess she doesn't like you, huh?"

Later, Toni was walking from one room to another and felt a small hand, most certainly a child's, grab her wrist and tug as if the child wanted some attention. When she stopped, the hand released her wrist.

The auditorium, also, has its share of activity. Jessie was conducting an EVP session when he heard dishes rattling on a table about fifteen feet away. He went to the table to see if he could determine the cause. The sound stopped. He examined the small stack of dishes and the table. Both seemed stable. Then he jumped up and down. Nothing happened. But when he went back to his equipment, the rattling started again. When he turned off his equipment and began packing up, the rattling stopped for good.

We spent several hours in the Opera House. Sue even bought a few things from Paula she absolutely couldn't resist. I just hope when we left, none of the spirits there attached themselves to Sue's "treasures" and followed us home.

West Central

Brooksville
May-Stringer House

Reddick
A Antique Mall

St. Petersburg Beach
Don CeSar Beach Resort Hotel

Tampa
Tampa Theatre

Wimauma
Redhawk Ranch

Ybor City
King Corona Cigars Café & Bar

CHAPTER 10

Redhawk Ranch
WIMAUMA

CHASING GHOSTS ACROSS THE LENGTH and breadth of Florida had been a thrill so far. I'd met dozens of wonderful people and had many exciting experiences, but like any road trip, it could wear you down. And after many weeks and hundreds of miles, I was getting tired and was thinking of taking a break from my travels. That's when I met Bud and Brenda Hoshaw of the Redhawk Ranch, five miles south of Wimauma. They invited me to their ranch and spiritual retreat center, and I quickly accepted.

From the moment I passed through the gates, I felt at peace, completely relaxed. But the tranquility and serenity of the place belies its violent past. Indigenous people occupied the area around Tampa Bay and the southwest coast of Florida for thousands of years. There is strong evidence that some of them lived on what is now the Redhawk Ranch. Tocobaga and Calusa tribes made their homes along the stream that flows along the south side of the retreat center.

The Calusa were powerful and dominated the area from just south of Tampa Bay to Fort Myers and inland to Lake Okeechobee. Their original name, Calos, meant "Fierce People," but they, as well as the Tocobaga to the north, were no match for the Spanish conquistadors who came into the area in the 1500s. Hernando de Soto, who landed in the Tampa Bay area in May, 1539, was especially brutal. De Soto's troops raped, murdered, mutilated, and slaughtered innocents with abandon. They even had trained greyhounds that attacked on command. The Spanish fed the dogs human flesh.

Smallpox, measles, and other diseases brought in by the Spanish further decimated the native peoples in the area. In time the land passed into the hands of white settlers, and the Indians were no more.

But something or someone wanted Native Americans back on the land. Bud and Brenda Hoshaw are Native Americans, Bud part Menominee and Brenda Cherokee and Cheyenne. The story of their acquisition of the 18.5 acres that is now the Redhawk Ranch is bizarre.

About twelve years ago, Bud and Brenda lived in a beautiful log home about four miles away. This house on five acres was their dream home, and they were quite happy. Then one day Brenda was on her computer when an advertisement for an 18.5-acre tract nearby popped up. She thought it strange, because she had been researching other things, not real estate. She deleted the ad and went back to work. The ad popped up again, and over the next ten days every time she went on the computer to Google something, the advertisement came up.

Bud and Brenda Hoshaw have made Red Hawk Ranch available for activities such as camping, meditation, and Native American ceremonies.

Finally, Bud told her, "Let's call the realtor. This obviously means something." And so they did.

Carl Weiss took them to the property on Route 579, which turned out to be hard to find, because the large "For Sale" sign had fallen over and couldn't be seen from the road. The frontage was completely overgrown and there was no drive into the place, although two rotting gate posts stood several yards off the road. But as soon as they stopped and got out of the car, Brenda knew she had to have the property. Brenda is psychic, and the first thing she saw was an Indian by the old gate posts. He seemed to be a sentry or lookout. And as they walked the property, she felt and saw other entities, including a red hawk. In the northeast corner, she was almost overcome by the beauty and peace of the place.

A bank in New York owned the property, and when Bud and Brenda discovered what the bank was asking, they were dismayed. They couldn't afford it. But Brenda prayed about it and knew they were supposed to be there, so they made an offer—one third of the asking price. The bank accepted their offer without even a counter offer. Stranger still, they discovered later that another man had gone around the realtor and directly to the bank with a much better offer and was refused.

Since moving onto the ranch, Bud and Brenda have encountered many entities and have the pictures to prove it. They have also made it available for camping, meditation, weddings, picnics, and Native American ceremonies. And, of course, they welcome paranormal investigators to come experience all the activity.

On one recent occasion, Brenda invited several sensitive friends down for an evening of "ghosthunting." Claire Castillo, Frank and Debbie Visicaro, Rick and Denise Incorvia, Cynthia Anderson, and Helen Bender all assembled with Bud and Brenda in their living room. They were asked to walk around the property without discussing their experiences and then write down whatever ever they saw, smelled, heard, or felt. After everyone was finished they would gather and tell the group what they had experienced.

Three hours later, they all returned to the living room, excited by what they had encountered. To begin, several of them felt that the whole area had once been underwater, and as geological changes had occurred, it had become dry land. There was also some sense that a stream once existed next to the driveway. They also felt that the stream running along the south side of the property had once been much wider and deeper.

Debbie and Rick agreed that this area had once been a village. They both had a vision of a panicked group of women, children, and old men getting into two canoes on the stream in the southwest corner of the ranch and fleeing. They felt that the village was under attack by white men. Not far away, several members of the group sensed a burial ground.

Farther upstream Brenda had a vision of an area where women gave birth. Possibly a hut of some kind once stood there. She said her knees went weak, and she had difficulty breathing. There was high energy all along the stream.

Frank also had a vision of several Spanish swords lying on the ground near the northeast corner in the vicinity of Bud and Brenda's Sacred Circle. He also saw what he thought was an angel, a wolf, and an owl, which he sensed were keeping them safe from deception. Near the creek he had the feeling that a child had drowned.

Denise and Bud saw a chief that was made of wood, its head covered with brightly colored wooden feathers. And almost everyone saw wraith-like wolves, eagles, coyotes, dragonflies, and even a white horse, in addition to the ghosts of two young white girls. Cynthia said she sensed a brave showing off the horse in a camp right behind the house.

On this occasion and many times before and since, Cynthia, Debbie, and Brenda also met an old man, a chief, sitting in a rocking chair on Brenda's porch. They smelled his pipe before they even saw him. He is a kindly person, and Brenda is comforted by his presence.

The group stayed late into the evening, sharing with each other. And although they each had different experiences, they all agreed that, except for the area where the burial grounds were located, the whole ranch was filled with positive energy.

On my visit, as usual, I saw nothing, but I was filled with peace and a sense of well-being. And I did have one experience. While walking into the Sacred Circle with Bud, the wind chimes hanging there began tinkling, which, Bud told me, almost always happened. Still, it made me smile.

After we soaked up the good vibes in the circle for several minutes, Bud motioned to me, "Come on. I want to show you something else."

And we walked out into a circle of trees in the center of the field which fronts the house. Bud produced a compass and handed it to me. When I stood exactly in the center of the ring of trees, the north arrow pointed north, but if I moved one step to the left, the needle swung left. If I stepped one pace to the right

Carved owls stand watch over Red Hawk Ranch, which is mainly a very peaceful place.

of center, it swung to the right. Very curious.

Bud and Brenda have several mastiffs for security. They are sweet dogs, but Bud is careful to pen them when strangers are around, because they are very protective. On my visit, Bud was with me when I got out of my truck, so all they did was lick my hand and vie for attention. I love dogs, and we made friends quickly. When I drove away from the house and stopped across the field at the Sacred Circle for one last look, the dogs came bounding after me, crowding around and begging for attention. When I finally walked back to my truck, opened the door, and started to step up, Butkus, their big male who doesn't weigh much less than his namesake, sat on my foot and looked up at me with soulful eyes. He didn't want me to leave.

"I know, pal. I don't want to leave either, but I've got to go."

With that he raised his rump and licked my hand goodbye.

Driving away, I laughed out loud with happiness, totally revived and ready to get back on my haunted road trip. The Red-hawk Ranch is a fantastic place, and when I finish with this book, I'm going back for a nice, long stay. I hope I can finally meet some of these friendly ghosts in person.

Spotlight on
Indian Spring Cemetery

Indian Spring Cemetery in Charlotte Harbor along Alligator Creek, about four miles south of downtown Punta Gorda, was established in 1886. Before it became a cemetery, the site was known as Indian Springs.

Charlotte Harbor was first settled by white men just after the Civil War, but archeological evidence shows that Calusa Indians—mound builders and seafaring warriors—occupied the area some three thousand years before. The creek provides access to what is now Charlotte Harbor, and there is a spring nearby with fresh water, so it would have been a suitable place to live. There is also evidence that there might have been an Indian burial ground nearby.

Scott Walker, founder of Peace River Ghost Tracker Investigations, has been through the cemetery and has reported all sorts of activity: lights moving across the graveyard and disappearing into graves, sounds of a woman crying, wailing voices that seem to be mourning a small child. Scott has also seen dark shadows that drift out of a mausoleum on the west side of the cemetery and fade out of sight in the tree line along Alligator Creek.

Jody* lives near the cemetery. We met her by chance in town, and when I told her I was looking for ghosts, she laughed. "We've got plenty," she said, and she proceeded to tell me about some of her experiences.

She and her mother used to walk their dogs in the evenings along the road next to the cemetery. One evening when she was about fourteen or fifteen, they walked a little farther than normal, and by the time they turned around to go home, it was getting dark. That didn't particularly bother them because they knew the area—this was their neighborhood. But as they strolled along, the dogs began to bark excitedly at something in the cemetery. At first Jody and her mother couldn't see anything, but then lights appeared, floating three-to-four feet off the ground, and occasionally what looked like large, dark balls of mist swooshed by them. Suddenly, the dogs stopped barking and became very nervous. Frightened now, they all raced home.

Jody doesn't walk there in the dark anymore. Occasionally, she hears wild noises coming from the cemetery, which she attributes to crazy teenagers. At least, she says she thinks they're teenagers. It helps her sleep better at night.

CHAPTER 11

King Corona Cigars Café & Bar
YBOR CITY

TEN YEARS AGO my ghost-magnet friend Joanne, Sue, and I went snooping around Ybor City, looking for ghost stories. Ghosthunting wasn't so popular then, and there weren't many resources to rely on. It was a hot day. As we ambled down Seventh Avenue, I spied King Corona Cigars Café & Bar and suggested we pop in for a beer—and air conditioning.

As soon as we walked in, Joanne got a tingling sensation, with goose bumps on her arms—and they weren't caused by the air conditioning. We struck up a conversation with the owner, Don Barco, and asked him about any unusual activities in the building. Don chuckled, "Actually, we do have ghosts here."

"Wait. Don't tell us," I replied. "Joanne is really sensitive.

Could we walk around a bit just to see what she might find?"

"Sure," Don said. "Let me show you the place, and I'll tell you a little of the history."

Joanne led the way, poking into nooks and crannies, while Don related the history of Ybor City and King Corona to Sue and me as we followed along.

Ybor City, now a neighborhood of Tampa, was founded in 1885 by a group of cigar manufacturers led by Vicente Martinez-Ybor, who wanted to move their cigar businesses from Key West to escape the high costs, labor strife, and transportation problems there. The Tampa area was an excellent spot: near enough to Cuba to get Cuban tobacco cheaply and easily; and with a new railroad line working its way across Florida, distribution of finished cigars across the entire United States would be possible.

Thousands of tabaqueros, tobacco workers, in Key West were recruited to come to Tampa for the chance to buy land and own their own homes, opportunities they never had in land-poor Key West. Señor Martinez-Ybor even built houses for his workers and sold them at a price just slightly higher than the building cost.

Ybor City was an immediate success. Tampa annexed it in 1887, over the protestations of Ybor himself, and by 1900 it had paved streets, brick buildings, a variety of fashionable shops, restaurants, street lighting, and a population of sixteen thousand. From its very beginning, it was a wide-open town.

A diverse population of Cubans, Italians, Spanish, Romanians, and Germans gave Ybor City an exotic, European atmosphere, which was enhanced by the many social clubs formed by the various ethnic groups. The Cuban Club, the German-American Club, the Italian Club, El Centro Español, among many others, all celebrating their own ethnic holidays and fetes, gave Ybor City an almost continuous party air.

The factories turned out millions of cigars a year. At one time Ybor cigar factories produced and shipped over five million cigars hand-rolled by skilled torcedores, and the money flowed. Clubs, restaurants, and bars were packed nightly, and the good times seemed never to end.

Prohibition in 1920, the Volstead Act, closed the taps on much of the alcohol across the country, but in Ybor City, with its tightly knit ethnic groups and clubs and numerous bars, the liquor still flowed freely. Speakeasies began popping up all over the town, and criminal elements soon took advantage of the loosely enforced regulations. Murders, muggings, and extortion were common. There were rumors of tunnels dug between buildings and across streets from one building to another, so that criminals might escape if a nightspot was raided.

With the stock market crash and the beginning of the Great Depression in 1929, lawlessness escalated. Hundreds were unemployed, and men were willing to do anything to feed and house their families. Bolita, an illegal game run by organized crime, became very popular. Charlie Wall, a notorious gangster, organized it into a huge, profit-making business and used the proceeds to invest into other questionable ventures. Corruption was rampant at all levels of government with rival gangs buying elections and competing with each other for control. The 1930s and '40s became known locally as the "Era of Blood."

Ybor City slowly deteriorated through the Depression years and the decades following until the 1980s, when an influx of artists looking for cheap and interesting studio space began moving in. Slowly, the once-empty buildings began filling with nightclubs, bars, and restaurants, and the crowds grew. Today Ybor City is thriving once again. On Friday and Saturday nights, Seventh Avenue is closed to vehicular traffic, and a carnival atmosphere prevails.

But there is a dark side to Ybor. The many years of turmoil and mayhem have left their mark. A medium once told my friend and Ybor City resident, Joe Howden, a thin black river of negativity flows beneath Seventh Avenue and affects everything that happens there. And there is a high level of paranormal activity throughout the area.

King Corona Cigars is no exception, but as Don was about to tell me something about the place, Joanne, who was leading us into the back hallway, stopped.

"Ugh," she called out, "There's blood back here. Something horrible happened!"

Don was at first alarmed. "What do you mean? Blood? Where?"

"No. I don't mean there's blood here now, but there was. Something really bad happened back here. Someone spilled a lot of blood. It's so negative!" Joanne turned to get away from the area.

"It could be," Don replied. "I've heard a lot of stories around Ybor. There's no telling what happened. Why don't we head up the stairs?"

Joanne and Sue started up to the next floor. Don continued telling me about the building. It had been a dress shop owned by Raul Vega for about sixty years. After the Vega years, it became an upscale women's store, La Nica Fashions, for another twelve. Then the building sat empty for about two years until Don opened King Corona Cigars.

Don's family has been in the cigar business for five generations, and he was anxious to renovate the building and open the store. But it needed a lot of work, so he enlisted the help of friends like Joe Howden and Joe's girlfriend at the time, Sarah. Joe, who is also an artist, has worked at the store ever since its opening and has his own tales to tell.

He was working late one evening, painting and installing display cases. Joe was by himself in the store, when he sensed that he was not alone. He didn't have any weapon except the hammer he was using, and the phones hadn't been installed yet. He looked around to see who was there and saw a very large man standing in the back of the store where the hallway is now located. Tensing, Joe tightened his grip on his hammer and started backing toward the front door. Just as suddenly as the man appeared, he evaporated.

On another occasion a few days later, Sarah was on a ladder painting the walls above the bar, when she saw a young girl in the back of the store. The girl was dressed in a long, old-fashioned dress and just stood there staring at Sarah. She called to the girl, with no response. Then, when Sarah started down the ladder to approach the young woman, she disappeared.

Don also has had his share of inexplicable experiences. He has felt many times that someone was watching him. He has heard voices and strange unidentifiable sounds, seen various people who have melted away right in front of him, and has walked into pockets of frigid air. Don mentioned that a medium once saw a man she believed to be Raul Vega walking around the store, and many customers have reported seeing strange people and feeling weird sensations from time to time, especially in the back of the store.

Don and I were just reaching the top of the stairs when we heard Joanne shriek. We hurried down the hall and into a storeroom, almost bumping into Joanne as she rushed out, Sue following.

Joanne was breathless. "There is a girl back there. She's cowering in a corner, and she is terrified. The energy is so negative I had to leave. She is absolutely petrified."

We tried to get Joanne to go back in to see if she could discover more details, but she refused. She was faint, so we went back downstairs and chatted for a bit while she collected herself. Finally, we said our goodbyes and left—going down the street for an excellent lunch at the Columbia Restaurant.

A few months ago as I was researching information for this book, I thought again about King Corona Cigars. Joanne was otherwise occupied, but I contacted another sensitive friend, Sheila Steen, and asked if she'd like to visit Ybor—I promised her a good lunch at the Columbia Restaurant.

When Sheila, Sue, and I walked into King Corona Cigars, we were welcomed warmly by Don and Joe. I hadn't seen either in several years, so we spent some time catching up. Then Don gave us another tour. I purposely hadn't told Sheila anything about the place and had asked her not to research it.

I was astonished. As we headed into the back hallway, Sheila said, "Oh, gruesome. Something bad happened back here. There's blood all over the place!" The same reaction Joanne had had ten years before. Don, Sue, and I were amazed.

Then we went up to the second floor and back into the storeroom. Again, Sheila found the same young girl Joanne had ten years before. The girl was cowering in the corner. She seemed lost, out of place. Sheila went into the corner under the staircase leading up to the next floor and squatted down for a few moments, then came back out.

"Oh, that poor girl. She was pleading, 'Por favor,' (please), and 'La gente no saben . . . ' (people don't know . . .)" Sheila felt an overwhelming aura of violence, terror, and secretiveness. She was as anxious as Joanne had been to leave the place.

Later, during lunch at the Columbia, we hashed over the events of the day. I felt sadness for the girl in the storeroom and was very curious about her fate. But I was also exhilarated that two different sensitives had had the same experience ten years apart.

CHAPTER 12

Don CeSar Beach Resort Hotel
ST. PETERSBURG BEACH

AFTER WE'D SAID OUR GOODBYES to Sheila, we drove
across the bay to St. Petersburg. I had made reservations at one
of Sue's favorite spots, the Don CeSar Beach Resort Hotel, which
coincidentally is considered quite haunted.

As we crossed the Intracoastal Waterway on Highway 682,
the "Pink Palace" rose out of the Gulf as if by magic. And, indeed,
the Don CeSar is a magical place. A combination of Old World
sophistication and Florida casual, its architecture is Mediterranean and Moorish. After we checked in, we went to the bar for a
drink before dinner. Sue was in heaven, reminiscing about the
last time we had stayed here.

We had come for a wedding, which was held on a beach-side patio. Afterwards, we had gone upstairs for cocktails. As Sue remembered, dozens of waiters seemed to float around the room with trays of champagne and delicious hors d'oeuvres. Then doors were flung open, and we entered the ballroom, floor-to-ceiling windows overlooking the Gulf and a spectacular sunset, for a lavish dinner. Waiters again drifted around the room discreetly filling water and wine glasses, clearing empty plates and dishes. And all the while a small orchestra played. After dinner and appropriate toasts, the bride and groom rose and danced across the floor. Sue had said, "This is so romantic!" I thought I was pretty smart to book us into the hotel again.

My focus at the moment, though, was ghosts. I had researched the paranormal activity and the history of the Don CeSar, but I wanted to talk to employees and anyone else who might have had personal experiences.

The story of the Don CeSar is a love story, and it began in the late 1800s in London. Thomas Rowe, a young American, was studying in England, and he loved opera. One evening while attending a performance of William Vincent Wallace's *Maritana*, the story of a young Spanish street singer who falls in love with a nobleman, Don César, Thomas was entranced by the beauty of the soprano who sang the title role. Lucinda de Guzman was herself Spanish, but of noble birth. After the last curtain fell, Thomas rushed backstage to see her, and when their eyes met, they fell in love.

Near the hotel where Lucinda and her parents were staying was a park with a secluded courtyard, a gurgling fountain in its center. Thomas and Lucinda met there whenever her parents were occupied and she was able to slip away from her *carabina* (chaperone). Lucinda was his Maritana, and he was her Don César. They made plans to elope, and Thomas arranged for a carriage to whisk them off to Southampton to board a ship for

America after the last performance of the opera. They agreed to meet at the fountain, the carriage waiting nearby.

But Lucinda's parents discovered their plot and confronted her in the wings as she was leaving the stage. They escorted her to the coast to sail back to Spain. Thomas waited all night in vain, not knowing what had happened to his beloved Lucinda. Brokenhearted, he returned to America. He never saw her again, but he never forgot her, and sent her many letters, which were always returned unopened.

Many years later, a British friend sent him a small package that contained a newspaper clipping and an envelope with a note inside. The clipping reported Lucinda de Guzman's death. The note was addressed to "My beloved Don César."

It read in part:

> ". . . We found each other before, and we shall do so again . . . Time is infinite. I will wait for you by our fountain . . . to share our timeless love . . . Forever. Maritana." (This excerpt is from Joel Sleed's Haunted Happenings.)

Thomas was by now a very wealthy man, having made a fortune in real estate. Devastated and sick at heart, his health failing because of an asthmatic condition, he went to Florida for the healing effects of the warm sunshine and fresh air. And Florida did improve his health and his disposition. He soon bought eighty acres on what was known as St. Pete Beach, accessible then only by a rickety toll bridge, and began building his dream, a monument to his lost Lucinda. It also happened to be the first luxury hotel on Florida's Gulf Coast.

With high ceilings, Italian chandeliers, French doors, marble floors, two swimming pools, terraces, patios, and balconies, the hotel exuded European splendor. In the lobby, Rowe also had constructed an exact replica of the fountain where he and Lucinda had carried on their ill-starred romance. He named the hotel the Don CeSar after the hero of the opera. One of the hotel restaurants was the Maritana Grill, and many of the streets in the area are still named after characters in the opera: Debazan Avenue, Maritana Drive, Don Jose Street.

During the three years of construction, Rowe could often be seen wandering around the site, dazzling in his white suit and Panama hat, talking to workers, encouraging them. And after the hotel was finished in 1928, he lived on the fifth floor and spent many hours sitting by the fountain in his replicated court-yard.

In spite of the Depression, the Don CeSar did well. Rowe lured the New York Yankees to St. Petersburg for the first spring training program in Florida, and the team stayed in the hotel. Because it was the only luxury hotel on Florida's Gulf Coast, it also drew celebrities, gangsters, and politicians from across the country. And there was a rumor that Rowe had hidden a very large sum of money in the hotel, which he used to supplement its sometimes meager earnings. In fact, legend says that Lucinda had warned him in a dream of the coming financial crisis, and this prompted him to set aside funds.

In any case, the Don CeSar survived until Rowe unexpect-edly died in the hotel in 1940. He had been in the process of changing his will so that his employees would inherit the facil-ity. Unfortunately, he hadn't signed it, so his ex-wife, Mary, inherited the Don CeSar.

Mary was not a good business woman and knew nothing about running a hotel. In a matter of months, the building fell into disrepair, and she finally lost it because she couldn't pay the taxes.

In 1942, the U.S. Government bought the hotel and turned it into a veterans' hospital and later a VA administration build-ing. The paintings, the carpet, all the luxurious furnishings, and Rowe's beloved courtyard and fountain were removed. The building remained in government hands until it was closed in 1967 and stood vacant, boarded-up, and forlorn except for vagrants and, according to some residents, mysterious happenings.

Some reported seeing the likes of Lou Gehrig, Al Capone, and other celebrities walking the beach at night. Others reported seeing strange lights and hearing the sounds of music and voices coming from the neglected patios and terraces.

As the old hotel continued to deteriorate with weeds growing in walkway cracks and trash heaping up, the city decided to demolish it and use the land for other purposes. Fortunately, a local group of history buffs saved the building in 1972 and began a multi-million-dollar restoration. The Don CeSar reopened in 1973, completely renovated and with Thomas Rowe's beloved fountain again replicated in the lobby.

After a lovely supper of Florida lobster tail and a nice bottle of cold, crisp pinot grigio to wash it down, Sue and I went for a stroll along the beach. It was beautiful, but we hadn't really talked to anyone yet about ghosts, so we finally went back into the lobby and started a conversation with two members of the hotel staff. They'd both had experiences of their own and lots of stories they'd heard from others.

At different times they'd both seen what they'd thought was probably a ghost, a woman dressed in a World War II nurse's uniform, watching them in the old kitchen. She had evaporated before their eyes. Neither staff member could understand what she might have been doing in the kitchen, but learned later that it had been a convalescent ward.

One of the men had also heard the story of a kitchen staffer who worked in the scullery, washing dishes. At one point late in the evening, he'd gone outside for a break, leaving a stack of dirty dishes piled in front of the dishwasher conveyor. When he returned, the dishes had been washed and stacked on a nearby table.

And many people have seen the chandeliers in the ballroom sway erratically, not moving in the same direction as if blown by the movement of air in the air conditioning system, but helter-skelter. "We've both seen that lots of time," one said, "but Thomas Rowe is our most famous ghost, if you want to call him that."

Many times a strange man in a white suit and Panama hat can be seen sitting on the steps overlooking the fountain. He seems to be lost in thought—or waiting for someone. And he has also been seen walking hand-in-hand with a dark-haired woman dressed like a gypsy. Could this be Thomas and his Maritana? They are seen walking the beach and terraces behind the hotel and also on the fifth floor.

After a lengthy conversation, our two friends decided they'd better get back to work. Sue and I had heard enough to confirm the research we'd already done, so, we set off again to enjoy the magic of the majestic Don CeSar. The next time we visit, we won't be chasing ghosts.

Spotlight on Island Hotel

Cedar Key is a really cool place. Old Crackers say that Cedar Key is like Key West was fifty years ago. I don't know, but I do know that, although I really love Key West, I'm always enchanted by Cedar Key, where Sue and I go often to rejuvenate. No laptops. No cell phones. We don't even watch TV when we're there. Just the two of us on a laidback island where time doesn't mean much, and what is happening in Washington or Wall Street doesn't have much relevance.

My friend Rosemary Norman and her husband feel the same way. Maybe we should have a "Pencil Head" thing like Key West enthusiasts have their "Parrot Head," since not so long ago Cedar Key was a major producer of pencils. Anyway, Rosemary, who is the founder of West Florida Ghost Researchers and an unusually sensitive person, has been to Cedar Key so many times and has had so many experiences, that she deserves to be named "Chief Ticonderoga."

On her first visit to Cedar Key—she and her husband had just discovered the island—Rosemary woke early on Sunday morning and decided to go for a walk. The weather was balmy with a gentle breeze blowing off the Gulf. Few people were about, and she was enjoying the morning. She walked down Second Street intending to turn right on A Street and walk around the pier. As she strolled along, she saw an attractive couple seated at a table across the street at the Island Hotel. The woman was wearing a beautiful, lavender dress and hat, the man a suit with a high celluloid collar. Both were nicely attired, but Rosemary thought it odd that their clothes looked as if they were from the Gay Nineties. Oh well, perhaps they were here dressed for a period event.

She waved to the couple. The lady smiled at her and raised her tea cup. Rosemary went on. After swinging around the pier, she decided that she'd go back up Second Street and down Third Street just to see the sights.

This time as she passed the Island Hotel, she saw no one. There was no table in front or any room for one, only dirt and broken concrete. Curious, she crossed the street and went into the hotel. No breakfast was being served; the dining room was closed. The receptionist sat half asleep at the desk. There was no activity at all. It was then that she realized she'd seen ghosts.

Rosemary and her husband have been back many times, and she has yet to see the lady in lavender. Still, she has always been satisfied. The island is so haunted, she has no problem running into spirits.

CHAPTER 13

Tampa Theatre
TAMPA

AFTER A LEISURELY BREAKFAST at the Don CeSar, we drove back across the bay to visit another of our favorite places, the Tampa Theatre, located on Franklin Street, just south of I-275. Franklin is not the most vibrant street in Tampa. Lined with office buildings and many closed businesses, it's a bit drab and dreary in some areas. But there is one bright spot, the Tampa Theatre, which fairly glitters, even on the outside.

Built in 1926 by the famous theater architect, John Eberson, in what was known as the Florida Mediterranean style of architecture, opulent is too weak a word to describe the theater. Floating clouds and ninety-nine twinkling stars covered the soaring ceilings. Mediterranean-style fountains, ornate statues—Christopher Columbus standing among Roman and Greek mythological characters—gargoyles, golden pillars, and plush velvet seats filled the auditorium. And, of course, there was the famous Mighty Wurlitzer Theater Pipe Organ with over fourteen hundred pipes. During the Great Depression, the Tampa Theatre was lavish beyond the wildest dreams of the moviegoers who came to escape the reality of their woes.

The theater did well for decades—until the 1960s and early '70s. Urban areas across the country fell on hard times then with many inner-city dwellers moving to the suburbs. The grand theaters of the 1930s especially were hard hit. Few people wanted to drive to a movie in town when they had so many entertainment alternatives in a nearby mall. As in many other places, the owners of the Tampa Theatre were considering demolishing the building and using the land for a more profitable enterprise.

In 1976, however, the city decided that the Tampa was too important a historical landmark to lose and bought the building. After a two-year, twenty-million-dollar restoration, the Arts Council of Hillsborough County took over management, and the theater today, looking just like it did in 1926, is one of the icons of Tampa. It is now on the National Register of Historic Places and is a Tampa City Landmark. The theater hosts classic, silent, and first-run films, concerts, special events, tours, and even a film camp and has an average annual attendance of 135,000.

Sue and I arrived mid-morning, and there were no scheduled events, so we were able to wander around the majestic theater in solitude to soak up the enchanting atmosphere of the place. We sat in the front row of the auditorium trying to recapture the excitement of watching a silent movie, listening to Rosa Rio playing the Wurlitzer. Rosa, who was born in 1903, has been an institution at the Tampa Theatre. She retired from playing only recently, after more than five decades, although she continues to consult on titles and musical scores that will be performed.

After enjoying the main floor for twenty minutes or so, we climbed the stairs to the balcony and the projection booth, where we sat waiting hopefully for an encounter with the Tampa's most famous spirit, Foster "Fink" Finley. Foster Finley was a projectionist, and he took his job seriously. Even though he never had to be at work until 1 P.M., he always took the bus and arrived at eight in the morning. He was a short, plump, balding man, but he dressed well, in a suit and tie. He might even have been considered somewhat of a dandy, the faint aroma of cologne wafting behind him as he walked. He looked like any other businessman on the street, and he was. His business was operating the projectors at the Tampa Theatre, and he never missed a day of work. But in 1965, after thirty-five years at the Tampa, Fink, a chain-smoker, suffered a heart attack in the projection booth and died two months later.

Shortly after Finley passed away, strange things began to happen at the theater. Bill Nelson, who had worked with Fink, went into the cramped projection booth and pulled the door shut behind him. Someone pulled back, and Nelson couldn't shut the door. Thinking another employee was playing games, he stepped out to see who it was. No one was there.

A generator room was located just off the projection booth. The door was kept closed because of the noise and heat from the generator. On many occasions, while the projectionists were busy with their machinery, the generator door would open of its own accord and then close again, as if someone were going in and out. That happens frequently to this day.

On another occasion one of the projectionists was sitting in the booth and watched the power switch flip off for no reason. No one was near the switch, which was in perfect working order. After several such occurrences, the projectionist left the theater and found work elsewhere.

One of the maintenance workers has had several inexplicable experiences over the years. Once he heard water running in the third floor shower and went up to turn it off. When he walked into the shower room, the shower was off. No one else was in there. Confused, he saw that the floor of the shower stall was wet, and he knew what he had heard. He shrugged and went back to work. Moments later, he heard the shower turn back on. This time when he entered, the shower was running, and, again, no one else was present.

Another time he was working on the main floor of the auditorium when he realized he'd lost his pocket knife. He had been on the stage the last time he remembered having it, so he searched there without success. Then he went all through the auditorium and finally the balcony. He never could find his pocket knife.

By then the presence of Fink's ghost was fairly well established, and someone suggested he ask Fink to return the knife. The worker went to the top of the balcony just below the projection booth and in a loud, clear voice requested that "Mr. Finley" return the knife, because he needed it badly. He stood quietly for a few moments and turned to leave. He looked down, and his knife was leaning against the wall right near his feet. Others have also lost items and found them again on the balcony or the mezzanine.

Tara Schroeder, the Tampa Theatre public relations manager, has had many encounters. Mostly, she hears keys jangling when she's alone in the building. Sometimes, Fink, or whoever the apparition is, gets theatrical and Tara hears chains being dragged. Others have heard the chains also. Moviegoers have reported seeing the faint image of some sort of apparition drifting across the stage in front of the screen during movies. And a woman in a white dress has been seen sitting in various seats on the main floor of the auditorium, only to vanish.

Many paranormal investigators have been through the building with EMF detectors, tape recorders, electronic digital thermometers, infrared cameras, and the like, and have captured many areas of dense electromagnetic fields, pockets of cold air, orbs, and strange smells.

As Sue and I sat in the projection booth, I began to notice a strange scent. It wasn't the heavy aroma of Old Spice, but it was vaguely familiar. Some of my friends from the Tampa Bay Ghost Watchers had told me about the strange aromas they'd noticed while going through the building. And Greg Jenkins in his excellent book, *Florida's Ghostly Legends and Haunted Folklore, Volume 1*, tells of his experience smelling the strange scent of a man's cologne or aftershave while he was watching a movie. Greg discovered later when he checked with his barber that he had smelled an old-fashioned "toilet water" still used today in some barbershops.

After we'd returned home, I checked Greg's book again. Lilac Vegetal. Toilet water. That's what he had smelled at the Tampa. Then I went to my barber. "Hey, Hank, have you ever heard of Lilac Vegetal?"

"Yup. Still use it. Got some right here."

I sniffed it. Yes. Same stuff that I had smelled in the projection booth.

In addition to the movies, concerts, and special events, the Tampa Theatre occasionally conducts Late-Night Ghost Hunts between 10 P.M. and 2 A.M. for small groups of people. None of my friends who've taken this tour have been disappointed. At the very least they capture orbs, strange sounds, unfamiliar aromas, and occasionally the sight of something or someone they can't quite make out. And almost always, the batteries in their electronic equipment go dead.

As Sue and I left to head back to Orlando, we looked over the schedule for the next few months and decided to come back in late August for a showing of the classic 1927 silent film *Metropolis*. We'll get to hear the Mighty Wurlitzer Theater Pipe Organ with its fourteen hundred pipes, and maybe the movie will coincide with a Late-Night Ghost Hunt. I'm already excited.

CHAPTER 14

May-Stringer House
BROOKSVILLE

I HAD HEARD that the May-Stringer House was extremely haunted. Its history was certainly full of tragedy. John May came from Alabama to Brooksville with his wife, Marena, and baby daughter in 1856. Brooksville was a sleepy little town then, nestled up against Fort DeSoto. May was an intelligent and industrious young man who quickly established a plantation and built a four-room house for his family. Within months he became one of the most successful plantation owners in Hernando County.

In 1857 Marena gave birth to another daughter, but tragically, John died of consumption in the house soon after. He was twenty-five. Marena, left with two babies and a large plantation to run, had little time for grief. Like so many of those early pioneer "cracker" women, she was tough and stepped right in with the work, finding the same success her husband had enjoyed.

For nine years she managed the plantation by herself until the end of the Civil War, when Frank Saxon, a wounded returning war hero, caught her eye. They married in 1866 and continued living in the house. Frank was variously the Brooksville Mayor, the Clerk of the Court, and the Chief of Police over the next several years.

In 1867 Frank and Marena had their first child, a boy, but he was weak and sickly from birth and died after five weeks. Distraught and grieving, they carried on with the plantation. Finally, in 1869 Marena gave birth again, this time to a girl, Jessie May Saxon—her middle name in memory of her mother's first husband. Again, tragedy struck. Days after the birth, Marena developed an infection, then called "child bed fever," and passed away. Frank was left with two stepdaughters and a baby, but he managed for three more years until 1872, when Jessie May also died.

Frank and his stepdaughters stayed on in the house for four more years until he married his second wife, Tulula Hope. Shortly thereafter, with so much death and tragedy connected to the home, he left it and built another.

In 1880, Doctor Sheldon Stringer bought the place and, over the next ten years, added another ten rooms, the house then appearing much as it is today. On the left side of the first floor is a foyer, which was the doctor's waiting room. His office and storage rooms were located behind that. On the right side of the house is a parlor, a dining room, and a kitchen. Upstairs are bedrooms on either side of a central hall. The original kitchen was separated from the house, but was moved forward and attached to the house in the 1930s by Doctor Stringer's granddaughter, Betty, the last Stringer to live there. Doctor Stringer also added a tower with four gables, so that the house now had seven gables; his favorite book was *The House of the Seven Gables* by Nathaniel Hawthorne.

Betty sold the house in 1950. It became a rental property, and then was abandoned and suffered heavy damage from vagrants. It was rescued by a concerned group of citizens in 1981 and became the Hernando Heritage Museum.

I first visited the May-Stringer House on Halloween during the annual fundraiser conducted by dozens of volunteers, serving as ghosts, goblins, and monsters. Two of the docents, Terri Miller, and her daughter, Amanda Mullen, gave me a personal tour. It was very entertaining—and crowded. Terri later told me they had over five hundred visitors that night. She invited me back for a quieter, more intimate tour.

Several days later I returned and was met by the ever-present Bonnie LeTourneau, Secretary of the Board of Directors, docent, and probably the May-Stringer House's most ardent supporter. Bonnie gave a great tour, explaining the history of the house in detail—but mostly she talked about the ghosts.

"Jessie May, Frank and Marena Saxon's daughter, is the official ghost of the house, but I think there are at least seven or eight more. Jessie May, her mother, and the Saxons' little boy, who would have been Jessie's half-brother, all died in the front bedroom upstairs. A funny story about Jessie May. You see those two tea cups on that small table in the parlor? We have a set of four but only put two out, because the table is so small. One day we opened up and there were three there. The next day all four, and they were helter-skelter, as a child might place them. Virginia Jackson, our chairwoman, was exasperated. 'Jessie,' she said sternly. 'There is not enough room on that table for four cups and saucers. We're going to have two on the table, and I'm taking the other two back upstairs to the storeroom. Do not bring them down again! Find something else to play with.' Those two cups and saucers have stayed on the table ever since, but a few days after Virginia's confrontation, the little figures in front of the fireplace in the dining room started being moved around."

As Bonnie explained, Dr. Stringer seems to be here, too. She has seen him on the front stairs; he is bearded and wearing a black coat. He doesn't do anything, just stands right below the landing, like he was shocked, seeing a badly injured patient down in the waiting room. He's probably just residual energy, but no one can explain it.

When the Stringers renovated, the doctor installed pocket doors in the dining room and parlor, so his family would have some measure of privacy. Many of the docents have seen a black mist crossing between the doctor's examining room and the parlor. Bonnie thinks that's Dr. Stringer also.

Bonnie continued her talk, "Then, there's James. That's what I call him. He was a World War I veteran who returned from the war to marry his childhood sweetheart, only to learn that she had already married someone else. Overcome with grief, he went to the attic and hanged himself."

Allegedly, James was a guest in the house and sleeping in the bedroom above the doctor's office. That's where he is encountered most often. But he moves throughout the house, and many people have seen him—the real estate folks across the street, the police, lots of visitors, and practically all the docents, of course. Not long ago a lady came through. She had lived here as a child when it was a rental. She and her sister were sleeping in the bedroom on the left upstairs, the one set up as a schoolroom now. Their bed was against the inside wall. She told the docent that in the middle of the night, she and her sister woke up to see a World War I soldier standing at the end of the bed.

James apparently likes the ladies. The docents get complaints from women all the time that someone pinched their bottoms. Usually they just apologize and move the tour on. Fortunately, James seems to be a kindly soul, and no one has ever been afraid of him.

"There is another soldier here, too, from the World War II. Not long after I started working here, a medium identified him, said he was looking for his dog that hadn't died when he was killed. I didn't believe in spirits then, but later, our curator found a diary of a soldier in the Canine Corps who was killed. His uniform is in the Military Room, the original kitchen where we have a display of uniforms."

In addition to Jessie May, there is at least one other girl here, a little older than Jessie. She has a doll that she is very protective of. When Bonnie first started doing these tours, she would pick the doll up to show it to people; it's very old. One day after a tour, her daughter, who was nine at the time, tugged her hand and said, "Mom, she doesn't want you to pick up her doll."

"What?" Bonnie asked.

"She doesn't want anyone to touch her doll."

"Oh." Bonnie finally understood and she hasn't touched it since. But others have and every time something bad happens.

"And then there's Mr. Nasty, the name we have given to this really mean entity that hangs out mostly in the attic upstairs and sometimes wanders down the back to the Military Room. I won't go near that attic anymore unless I absolutely have to. He hit me once and I just freaked out, screamed at him that he was not to touch me, that I was going to be in this house whether he liked it or not. So he'd better play by my rules. Then I was going up the back stairs and got this pretty stout tap on the head, as if he were saying, 'No. No. No. I make the rules.' Since then I stay out of his way and he stays out of mine."

"There are probably more spirits. We have over ten thousand

donated items, so it stands to reason that some things, perhaps like the soldier in the Canine Corps, will come in here attached to the artifacts."

The tour was finally finished. I had been mesmerized for almost three hours by Bonnie's stories, but it was time to go. As I was leaving, I asked about the night-time ghost tour.

"Oh, by all means. Come. I'll guarantee you a good time, and you might get to experience a few things yourself."

I began thinking. Wouldn't it be interesting to bring a few of my sensitive friends along, just to see what might happen? Bonnie thought that was a great idea, and so it was arranged.

As soon as I got home I started calling people. Claire Castillo, Sheila Steen, Joanne Maio, Cynthia Anderson, Minda Stephens, and Casey McCarthy all agreed to come. The following Friday evening, which happened to be Friday the thirteenth, we met Bonnie, Terri, and Amanda in the parking lot. This was going to be exciting.

Even before we started, Sheila, who had never been in the house and was the "blind," related that two days before, she started having visions of the place and described the foyer and staircase accurately, even the storeroom under the stairs. We were all amazed.

Casey escorted Sheila and Minda, who also had never been there, on a tour, just to get their initial impressions. Then the rest of us followed.

As the evening progressed, my sensitive friends identified all the known entities in the house, although no one actually saw any spirits. Although ghosts can manifest themselves anywhere, they seem not to be able to do so around very many people, perhaps because the needed energy is more quickly depleted when in contact with other people's bioelectric fields.

In the doctor's office is a very old wooden wheelchair. Years before, Bonnie's daughter saw the bottom half of a Confederate soldier in the chair and sensed that he had died of gangrene. On this evening as we entered the room, both Cynthia and Joanne immediately commented on the awful smell emanating from the chair. Sheila smelled it and told us that from her past experience, that particular smell was always associated with gangrene. A few minutes later Joanne saw a small pile of human limbs on the porch by the outside door to the examining room.

Upstairs in the attic Mr. Nasty made his presence felt; we all got headaches, but James also seemed to be present, protecting us. In fact, he and Minda, who was using dousing rods, started a little flirtation that continued throughout the evening in the rest of the house.

As we wandered in small groups through the various rooms, we saw black mists, heard strange noises, and were touched on our shoulders—I think Minda even got pinched. In the Military Room and in the schoolroom, James's former bedroom, Sheila heard a man's voice saying "rendezvous with one and only." That must have been James, thinking about his lost love.

Nearing midnight, we all gathered in the dining room, and Terri turned on an old Victrola, which played cylinders. A growling sound immediately came from somewhere near it, and as we looked back into the kitchen toward the Military Room, we noticed it becoming black as night, even though there was plenty of light from the outside shining in through the many windows. Almost simultaneously, our cameras and recorders went dead, except for Claire's camcorder. When she looked at her pictures the next day, she discovered traveling orbs zipping all around the Victrola.

Time to go. We congregated in the parking lot, while Terri and Amanda locked up. We were all tired but exhilarated. Bonnie was right. Mr. Nasty, James, and all the others had given us a spectacular ghosthunting road trip.

CHAPTER 15

A Antique Mall
REDDICK

IN MY SEARCH FOR HAUNTED PLACES, I discovered A Antique Mall on the Internet and called Mr. Warren Keene, the owner, to question him about it. "Sure, we got ghosts; we must have. Someone's been hittin' the till, and it ain't me." He went on to tell me the story of the Barnum murders, which occurred in the store, and as much as he knew about Lewis Barnes, the convicted murderer. "Come on up and check the place out—maybe I can sell you something."

Time for a road trip. My spooky pal, Joanne, her daughter, Gwyneth, and I jumped into my truck and headed up I-75 to Exit 368. Gwyneth kept track of our mileage and generally kept us in stitches with her eleven-year-old jokes.

Surrounded by pasture land and forests, A Antique Mall is

fifteen or twenty miles from nowhere. Even though it sits on a knob overlooking Interstate 75 and is just ten feet from the I-75 boundary fence, it is a lonely place—especially at night. The road into the place would tax a Humvee, but the building itself is immaculate and well-maintained. Not only is it huge, perched on its hill, it is also bright barn red. You can't miss it. We arrived in the late afternoon, parked the truck, and entered. Mr. Keene was sitting behind the counter, and we introduced ourselves.

"Ah, the ghosthunters," he said, shaking my hand.

We exchanged pleasantries, and then I asked if he'd ever seen or heard anything. He hadn't but said some of his employees had heard people talking back around the loading dock when no one was there. "They might just be pulling my leg, though."

When Joanne and I go to potentially haunted sites, we both agree that she won't research beforehand, and I won't tell her anything I know about the places. So I hadn't related to her any of the details Mr. Keene had told me on the phone and what I had gleaned from the Internet, and I could see she was anxious to explore the store.

We chatted a few more minutes, thanked Mr. Keene again, and then started our walk through the mall. Gwyneth and I followed Joanne to watch her reactions as we slowly moved up and down the aisles, working our way from the front of the store to the back. It was like following someone through a minefield, waiting for the lead man to get blown up. Back and forth, up and down through the aisles, walking slowly and quietly.

Then we reached the stairs. Joanne froze. "Someone was here, right there on those first steps next to the banister on the right side. A man and a woman, and they were scared, really terrified."

I didn't say anything as we skirted around to the left side and proceeded up the stairs. Joanne kept looking back at the bottom right side of the staircase. The second floor above the stairs is open, more of a balcony with a railing around it. When we got to the top, we stopped and Joanne looked around. Again, she froze. "There are two men over there on the far side of the balcony."

"Are you sure?" I asked. During my research, I had discovered only one possible male ghost, the man with the woman on the stairs.

"Yes, I'm sure. They don't frighten me, but they're there, and they're pretty nasty," she replied, and we moved on around the balcony to where she'd seen the men. She felt nothing. "Hmm," she said. "I know I saw something over here."

We stood there a while, waiting for something else to happen. It never did, so we moved on, looking around the front of the store on the second floor. I had read about an antique dresser in the front on the second floor and a little girl playing in the area. Psychics, mediums, and other sensitive people supposedly see her, and others who might not see her at least feel a presence and a coldness in the area. I didn't say anything to Joanne but looked around for the dresser. It was gone, and Joanne didn't sense a thing.

We continued up and down the aisles, making our way to the back of the second floor without encountering anything, although Gwyneth and I were a little spooked and stayed pretty close behind her mother. The second floor yielded nothing more, except the two men Joanne had first seen.

With not a little trepidation, I followed Joanne down the stairs, staying to the south side, of course, away from the couple on the bottom steps. We'd been in the store almost an hour, and from my previous research, I was well aware of what we might find in the back of the store. We turned and headed that way, my eyes glued on Joanne to see her reaction. The sun slipped toward the western horizon outside as twilight approached, and I realized no one else was in the mall except Mr. Keene, who obviously had closed up, but graciously hadn't interrupted us.

We circled through several large pieces of furniture in the back left corner and didn't feel anything, and then we turned slowly toward the back right corner where a walk-in safe stood. I waited, not saying anything. Joanne stepped forward into the safe and gasped, clutching her chest. I could see that she could hardly breathe as she jumped back out.

"Oh, that is evil! The energy is so heavy in there! Someone was murdered in there. You can just feel their terror." Then she walked out toward the loading dock and came back quickly, shaking her head. "That is not good out there, either."

We hurried back toward the middle of the store and stopped for a minute to compose ourselves, Joanne catching her breath and Gwyneth looking worried. When we had all calmed down, I related the story Mr. Keene had told me and the other facts I had learned from my research.

One June afternoon in 1984, Lewis Barnes and a Mexican companion entered the store, then known as Wayside Antiques. No one else was there except the owners, Betty and David Barnum. Barnes and his partner said hello, then began looking over the items and selecting several high-end pieces. When they had finished, the bill came to a quarter of a million dollars. Barnes told them that he was a dealer from out West and spoke the language of the trade, asking them what was the best they could do, but otherwise not haggling over the price of any of the pieces. The men were well-dressed and pleasant enough, so the Barnums had no reason to be suspicious. Barnes then told them that he would need to get his truck but would return by the close of business, six o'clock, or shortly thereafter. They must have been delighted by their good fortune and not minded waiting a bit.

The Barnums closed the store at six and waited for their wealthy customers from out West. About six-thirty Barnes and his friend reappeared with a large truck, backed up to the loading dock at the rear of the store and out of sight from I-75, and began loading the furniture and other items Barnes wanted.

Betty and David helped with the loading, but Barnes was very meticulous, not wanting to damage any of the merchandise, so they were still loading as the sun set. When they were nearly finished, suddenly, without warning, Barnes and his Mexican friend pulled out guns. They forced the Barnums to sit on the stairs leading to the second floor, where they handcuffed the couple to the iron railing and gagged them, then finished loading their truck. When they were ready to leave, they went to the front counter, emptied the cash register, and came back to the Barnums still handcuffed to the stairs. Betty and David must have been terrified. Barnes ushered them to the walk-in safe at the rear of the building. In court testimony he stated that he had meant only to lock them in but that his partner looked at the couple sitting petrified on the safe floor and shot both of them in the head.

The two men then drove to Las Vegas and sold the entire lot of antiques to a Mr. Edwin Slade for eighty-five hundred dollars. Slade enlisted the help of his daughter and her boyfriend, and the five unloaded the truck, storing the items in Slade's house. When they finished, Barnes and the Mexican disappeared.

Slade made a big mistake asking his daughter's boyfriend to unload the truck, revealing his illicit activities to the young man. A month later Slade and the boy argued, and the boyfriend reported the stolen goods to the police. Slade most certainly knew the items had been stolen but wasn't involved in the murders and was never charged. Months later, Barnes was tracked down, arrested, and convicted of the theft and murders. His Mexican compatriot was never found.

As I finished the story, Mr. Keene came back to see how we were doing, and we walked back to the front of the store to leave. When we got to the checkout counter, Gwyneth laid down a hair clip she wanted, and I handed him a 1907 edition of a book of Robert Service poetry I had discovered.

"Ah, good. You're buying. You know you can't leave if you don't buy something, and if you do sneak out, I'll send my ghosts after you."

We laughed, paid for our purchases, and thanked him profusely. When we got outside, Joanne laughed again and said, "I wouldn't mind the Barnums following us home, but I do not want those nasty guys upstairs anywhere near me."

Driving back to Orlando as the twilight darkened into evening, we rehashed the day. It was a good road trip.

East Central

Daytona Beach
Pinewood Cemetery

Longwood
Longwood Village Inn

Orlando
Orange County Regional History Center

Sanford
Page Jackson Cemetery

CHAPTER 16

Orange County Regional History Center

ORLANDO

ORLANDO WAS A COW TOWN in the middle of cow country in 1857 when it first became the seat of Orange County. Florida, especially isolated central Florida, was quite lawless then. The Third Seminole War didn't end until May 1858, and those who chose to live here were a pretty rough lot. Benjamin Caldwell, an Alabama man who owned considerable land in central Florida, donated four acres for the site of the county courthouse, a square bounded by what would become Magnolia Avenue, Central Avenue, Court Street, and Wall Street.

Courthouse Square was the center of town and quickly became the focal point of activity. The first courthouse was a simple log structure built on the site in 1863, and it certainly provided much entertainment, as cattle rustlers and highwaymen were brought to justice and tried there. This courthouse burned down in 1868. Some believed it was set aflame by cattle rustlers whose cases were due to be tried. The fire destroyed the records as well as the building, so the cases never came to trial.

The next two buildings were of frame construction, the second a two-story structure built in 1869 and replaced by a three-story courthouse in 1875. The second, and presumably the third, also served as church, schoolhouse, dance hall, and general assembly. Both were moved and replaced in 1892 by a red brick Romanesque Revival edifice that became an iconic symbol of Orlando civic pride, much as the Lake Eola fountain is today.

By the 1920s, Orlando had grown dramatically, and it was time to replace the old courthouse with a newer, larger building, although the "Red Brick Courthouse" wasn't actually torn down until 1958. In 1927 the county built a new structure just north of the square on land purchased from the adjacent Episcopal Church. Built in the Neo-Classical Revival style, which was waning in popularity, its architecture was outdated from the beginning but was no less significant. It was a magnificent building with two courtrooms, jury rooms, and a jail on the fifth floor that could house up to 132 inmates. During its seventy-odd years of service as a courthouse, before it was replaced in 1998 by the present courthouse three blocks north, it witnessed some of the most chaotic events in our history: the Great Depression,

World War II, the Korean War, desegregation, the Vietnam War, and many prominent court cases, the most famous of which was the Ted Bundy murder trial.

Bundy was one of the most notorious serial killers in the twentieth century. No one knows for sure how many women he raped and murdered or even when he began his decades-long spree. Several times he was apprehended and convicted, only to escape. He was finally caught and convicted in 1979 of the murders of several Florida State students and was given a death sentence. While on death row in 1980, he was tried again in the Orlando courthouse for the abduction, rape, and murder of twelve-year-old Kimberly Leach in Lake City. Once more convicted and sentenced to death, he was eventually electrocuted on January 23, 1989, at the Florida State Prison in Raiford.

Fast forward to 2009. The old courthouse had become the Orange County Regional History Center. Kissimmee Paranormal Investigations was preparing to conduct an investigation of the Center. Lois Lee, a psychic and paranormal investigator, entered the History Center with high expectations. Previous paranormal excursions had discovered several entities.

In Court Room A, Lois wandered around for some time and then sat in a chair at the defense table. Not thinking of anything in particular, she dropped into a trance-like state and her breathing became heavy and fast. She began experiencing emotions of fear and anger, and she felt her chair being bumped forward. Her teammates started asking her questions, but she was incoherent. At one point she screamed in terror, "I didn't do it! I didn't do it," but at the same time thinking that "he" did do "it," whatever "it" and whoever "he" was.

Then inexplicably she felt her hands and legs beginning to tingle and start to go to sleep. The tingling, buzzing sensation became so severe that she felt her circulation was completely cut off, and she gasped something unintelligible about being handcuffed. She began pounding her hands on the table to bring back the circulation, but the sensation spread through her whole body. Sharp, excruciating pains jabbed her sides, and she shouted, "Let go! Let go! Let go!" Now much alarmed, her teammates grabbed her and escorted her out of the room into the hallway, where she shook her hands and stomped her feet to bring back the circulation.

Lois never did learn who "he" was, but she doesn't rule out the possibility that it might have been someone who had experienced an electrocution. It might even have been Ted Bundy, whose name is carved on a corner of the desk at which she was sitting.

When a local radio station was housed across the street from the courthouse, employees working late in the evening often reported lights moving around, shouts, moans, cell doors slamming, and maybe even the sound of what might have been gunfire; there had been shootings at the courthouse before. None of these reports were verified, however.

Other paranormal investigators have had contact with a male presumed to be a lawyer, who paces back and forth in Courtroom A. Some have encountered two entities, one of whom might be a judge and another who might actually be Ted Bundy. The jury foreman's chair also sometimes turns and faces whoever is walking about the courtroom.

Just as in our present courthouse where space has been set aside for the children of witnesses, defendants, and observers, similar accommodations were made in the old courthouse by using the Jury Room just across the back hall from Courtroom A when it was not otherwise occupied. In the Jury Room, many have met Emily, a little girl who apparently spends most of her time there but has, on occasion, been seen in the hallway between the Jury Room and Courtroom A and in other areas. She is apparently a sweet child who likes to play. Some have brought toys for her and have reported actually interacting with her as she plays.

Others have also reported a dour woman and a man thought to be a bailiff in the Jury Room, both of whom try to stay in the background. Perhaps they were there to supervise the children or to assist the jurors sitting in session.

On her first visit, when Lois had experienced the electrocution, she also got a fleeting glimpse of Emily at the entrance to the courtroom. But the child almost instantly vanished when two of Lois's team members came into the room. Lois also picked up a male who might have been the lawyer others had experienced, but that contact, too, was fleeting.

On her second visit some of the other investigators reported a male presence in the Jury Room, so Lois went in and sat down, waiting for something to happen. Soon she sensed a man she thought to be a lawyer. He seemed to be a contented, middle-aged man probably from around the 1930s. He wore a white fedora and glasses. Lois described him as "respectably round." He was at first reluctant to make contact, but as she spoke softly to him, he gradually moved closer, at one point setting off a motion detector. That alarmed him, and he wanted to know what the "contraption" was. Lois explained that by waving his hand in front of the EMF meter, he could make the lights flash up and down and in that way communicate with them.

By asking a series of questions, she learned a little about him. Either his name was Clay or he was from Clay County; he wasn't very clear about it. He was a gentle man who enjoyed fishing, but not golf, during his lifetime. And he was a defense lawyer who was proud that he'd kept more innocent people out of jail than he'd gotten guilty parties acquitted. He didn't have any contact with the other spirits in the area, and he didn't like to be around people. During the evening ghost tours in the museum, he often hid in the Jury Room.

Joanne, my ghost ferret, Sue, and I visited on a cold, dreary, December day. The Center was quiet. While Sue and I interviewed Ms. Cynthia Melendez, the Curator of Collections, and Dr. Tana Porter, the Research Librarian, Joanne wandered around. Later over lunch at the Daily News down the street, Joanne shared the paranormal activity she had experienced.

She had gone first to Courtroom A and sat quietly in several locations. She didn't encounter much. The judge's bench was highly energized, but she had found nothing specific. The same was true at the defendant's table where Ted Bundy's name is carved. Lots of energy surrounded the area, but there was nothing specific or intimidating.

However, in the Jury Room she came across a tall, slender man with dark hair and a moustache. He did not interact with her in any way but paced back and forth, appearing to be deep in thought. Joanne sensed that he was probably a lawyer and was considering a case he was involved in. He was definitely not the talkative, stout fellow Lois Lee had encountered earlier.

On the fourth floor, Joanne met a little girl in a pinafore sitting on the steps of the Cracker cabin there. She was about six years old and seemed to be very happy, playing quietly by herself. Joanne wasn't able to engage the little girl, who might have been Emily, the child others had seen in the Jury Room and Courtroom A, but she watched her for several minutes.

Joanne found nothing else, but considering it was daytime with much activity going on, it was probably a wonder that she experienced anything at all.

The Orange County Regional History Center is still one of the finest buildings in Orlando and an excellent museum. Let's hope the ghosts there appreciate it as much as those still living do.

CHAPTER 17

Longwood Village Inn
LONGWOOD

MY DIRECTIONALLY IMPAIRED PAL, Joanne, got lost one day driving down I-4 and ended up in Longwood, a few miles north of Orlando, at the Longwood Village Inn. Not at all shy or retiring, she went inside to ask directions and quickly became friends with Ann Biedenharn, the agent liaison for Lenny Layland of Homevest Realty, which owns the nineteenth-century building. And, as it turned out, the Inn, now an office building, is quite haunted.

When Joanne finally found her way home, she called, excited. After she told me what she'd found, I was excited as well, so we phoned Ann to ask if we could come up and go through the place. Ann graciously agreed. "Of course. Whenever you like."

The next day Joanne, daughter Gwyneth, and I were greeted with a huge smile and warm welcome from Ann. She had prepared an extensive history and summation of the paranormal activity there, but wanted us to walk around first to get unbiased impressions.

The building has three stories, with a two-story addition built on the back and a deep porch on three sides. Wide staircases on either side of an expansive, bright, and airy lobby lead to the second and third floors, lending a sense of openness and space.

While I chatted with Ann, Joanne meandered around the lobby, occasionally calling out to me about what she was experiencing. She walked back to the ladies' room just past the reception desk and yelled at me, "You gotta see this." Of course, I couldn't "see" what Joanne was looking at, but I went over to her anyway. "There's a guy standing right here. He's tall and thin with short gray hair, and he's wearing a dark business suit. He looks like he's listening intently to you and Ann, like he's jealous or something." I glanced at Ann. She was smiling to herself.

A few minutes later the man seemed to have wandered away, so we ascended the left staircase. All the way up, Joanne was "oohing" and "ahing" about the energy she was feeling. On the second floor she stopped and looked out the back window to the roof. "I'm not quite picking it up, but there's something about that roof. Weird."

We stood a few moments then climbed to the third floor and ran into another area of concentrated energy. Joanne described it as feeling like a shot of Novocain. With me in tow she rushed forward and stopped again in front of a suite of rooms, 308, 309, and 310. All three were empty except for some office furniture in the middle room, 309. Joanne entered Room 308. Immediately, her breathing became labored. "Oh, I feel like I've been running for miles," she gasped and hurried out of the room. The energy wasn't negative, but it was intense. She re-entered the room one more time, then went through the adjoining door to Room 309.

At once she confronted a male presence who didn't seem to want us there at all. Joanne sensed that he was telling us to leave. Again, this entity wasn't menacing; he just wanted us to know that this was his space, and he wanted his privacy. He was upset also about the furniture being there. Since this room belonged to him, he wanted the furniture removed, Joanne thought.

In the next room, 310, she sensed a formless presence. As Joanne walked around the room, she got a little jolt every time she stepped on a squeaky floor board. Soon, her eyes began to burn. Something or someone in the room was not happy she was there.

Back in the hallway we started down the right-hand staircase, again encountering energy all the way to the first floor. Joanne ducked into a windowless conference room just off the lobby and sat in a chair at the head of the expansive table for a few minutes. She felt nothing, so she joined Ann and me at the reception desk. Soon she headed back to the conference room. This time she noticed that a chair at one side of the table had been pushed back, as if someone wanted her to sit there. She did so. As she sat quietly, she noticed something glowing next to her. It was a man's trouser leg, just the calf. The rest of the "man" she sensed more than saw. It was the same tall, thin man she had encountered near the ladies' room. He was standing barely five inches away and was staring across the room, not speaking or moving. After several minutes Joanne rose to get me. When we returned, the man was gone.

We went back to the main desk to talk to Ann. "And, what did you find?" Ann asked. After Joanne told her what she had experienced, Ann laughed and said, "You're pretty good. The man you saw by the ladies' room we've named George. We think he was a previous owner. And I can tell you, he likes women. That's also who you met in the conference room. Several sensitive people have been through here, and they always feel a lot of energy on the stairs."

Ann had much more to tell us. Not long before our visit, a young man came into the building to tell her what had happened to him the night before. He and two friends were driving by the back of the building about ten o'clock and saw a man in a three-piece suit standing on the second floor roof. Alarmed, they stopped and started yelling at the man, "Don't jump! Don't jump!" He continued to stand there, so they rushed down the street to the police station for help. When they came back with a policeman, the man had disappeared. The officer just shrugged, "This place is haunted. It was probably the ghost." Maybe the ghost Joanne had seen by the ladies' room? And the incident explained her "weird" feeling when looking out at the roof.

Ann herself spent a night in the building with two other women, a kind of adult slumber party. They didn't see any ghosts, but the photographs they took showed many orbs. And about four in the morning, they were lying in their sleeping bags talking quietly when a man's voice said very plainly, "You gotta believe!" They almost jumped out of their skins, only to start laughing.

Another evening Ann was doing some work for a tenant on the third floor—and of course, it was a dark and stormy night—when she heard what sounded like a tea cart rolling down the hall. Ann knew she was alone in the building. She looked out in the hall. It was empty. Then, the thought struck her. Room service! Was this a ghostly bellman bringing dinner? She got goose bumps, grabbed her purse, and sailed out the door and down the stairs.

Ann's most exciting experience occurred one afternoon about two-thirty. She noticed a glowing light on the far wall (north) near the ceiling. The building faces southeast, so it couldn't have been the reflection of the sun from a building across the street. At that moment two ladies came out of one of the offices on the first floor, saw the glow, and asked what it was. Just as Ann said she didn't know, a form started taking shape in the middle of the glow. The three women could tell very plainly that it was a child with short hair. Later they all said that they couldn't determine the gender, but they were adamant that it had a child's face. Suddenly, the glowing light and the figure flew off the wall and dissipated into nothing in the middle of the lobby. The three women screamed and ran out the back. This sighting occurred only once, but Ann remembers it as especially unnerving.

Occupants of the building have heard footsteps along the third floor. The elevator sometimes operates by itself. Figures have been seen in windows when the building has long been closed and locked. And the police occasionally respond to the burglar alarm but never find any evidence of forced entry. Many a veteran police officer will readily admit that the Longwood Village Inn is haunted.

Mr. Josiah Clouser built the three-story, luxury Waltham Hotel, which eventually became the Longwood Village Inn, in 1883. One of the finest hotels at the time, it boasted indoor bathrooms and electric room-service bells. Rooms cost a pricey three dollars a day.

In 1922, George Bunker-Clark bought the building, renovated it, and reopened it as the St. George Hotel. Sadly, less than a year later in April 1923, Bunker-Clark died in an accident at the rear of the hotel while hosting an ice cream social there for the community. The building remained a hotel for some time, but has also housed a gambling establishment, a movie set, a flop house, a junk car lot, and a baseball umpires' school—George Barr built a two-story addition on the back of the building for locker rooms and showers in 1952.

The Longwood Village Inn is one of the oldest three-story wooden nineteenth-century hotels in Florida and is on the National Registry of Historic Places. It is definitely haunted, but I can attest to the fact that there is a sense of calm in the building. Maybe charming George is the influence.

Spotlight on Cassadaga

Cassadaga, Florida, is like no other small town in America. There are no banks, no drugstores, no laundries, no gas stations. There are few people wandering about and no children playing in the streets. It is almost unearthly quiet, and that's the way the townspeople like it.

George Colby, a New York medium, was led by his spirit guides to Florida to establish a spiritualist camp at Cassadaga in 1875. Mr. Colby, suffering from tuberculosis when he arrived, found the waters at the site he chose to be soothing. He later was completely cured. The Cassadaga Spiritualist Camp quickly became an educational center where Spiritualism could be taught unhindered by outside interference. The oldest active religious community in the United States, Cassadaga is now a mecca for spiritualists, mediums, astrologers, and psychics.

The humdrum activities, sounds, and sights of a normal small town may be missing in Cassadaga, but spirits are here. The air in this tiny town off I-4 between Orlando and Daytona fairly shimmers with energy. Visitors can find almost any sort of spiritual counseling they want. Black magic and witchcraft are not used.

Of course, Cassadaga has its hauntings. The most famous are found at the old Spanish-style Cassadaga Hotel. Arthur, an Irish tenor, lived at the hotel for a time and died there in the 1930s. He is occasionally seen in the hallways by guests, and he will answer questions by flipping lights on and off. Arthur lived there in the days before air conditioning, and his room, number 22, smells of body odor. It also smells of cigars and gin, which Arthur apparently enjoyed.

Or did those aromas come from Gentleman Jack, another entity often reported? No one seems to know now where he came from or very much about him, but he also supposedly haunts the hotel along with two little girls, Sarah and Katlin, who frolic up and down the halls.

Whether you stay in the hotel or come only for the day, Cassadaga is worth a visit just to enjoy the quiet and feel the incredible energy of the town.

CHAPTER 18

Page Jackson Cemetery
SANFORD

RICH CIRONE LED OUR LITTLE CARAVAN off the highway and into the complex of Sanford Cemeteries. Rich and his wife, Kim, who is very sensitive, are the founders of Kissimmee Paranormal Investigations (KPI) and had agreed to run an investigation of the Page Jackson Cemetery in Sanford for my benefit.

Page Jackson is one of five cemeteries in the complex and is considered to be the most haunted. In 1870 General Henry Sanford, through his London-based Florida Land & Colonization Company, bought over twelve thousand acres of land near Lake Monroe and laid out the community of Sanford, which was incorporated in 1877 with a population of about one hundred.

Page Jackson Cemetery, along with the others in the complex, was established about that time.

Officially, it was named the Odd Fellows Cemetery. William Page Jackson farmed five acres adjacent to the cemetery and dug the graves. As funeral processions entered the area, Mr. Jackson would always wave and offer his condolences. Over the years, residents began referring to the cemetery as the "Page Jackson," and that is how it is known to this day.

Joanne, Sue, and I had already visited Page Jackson in daylight a couple of days before to familiarize ourselves with the site. The place is spooky in the daytime—I could only imagine what it would be like at night. Some of it is cleared, but there are many areas overgrown with thick brush that are almost impenetrable. Above-ground tombs dot the cemetery, and there are several family plots surrounded by old, iron fences, some terribly neglected. There are also stands of live oaks bearded with Spanish moss. Even during the day, the effect of all this is one of gloom and foreboding.

During our daylight walk-through I was expecting at least a certain amount of paranormal activity. The week before I had met Kevin Young in the neighborhood adjacent to the cemetery, and when I asked, he had quite a story to tell. He had moved into a new house on the street just to the east of the cemetery. At first, he didn't even know a cemetery existed so close to his house because of the dense foliage along the eastern boundary of Page Jackson. But shortly after moving in, he was outside on his porch late one evening and heard strange noises coming from the woods. When he looked in that direction, he saw greenish glowing lights, moving through the brush and he heard hollow-sounding moans. Unnerved, he went back inside. Since that first night, he has heard the eerie noises and seen the strange lights regularly. His neighbors have told him that there are restless spirits that wander the cemetery at night. He did say that vandals sometimes enter and deface the graves, but he is convinced that Page Jackson is haunted. Even though an occasional police car or caretaker patrols the cemetery, Kevin Young will not enter, night or day.

So, based on Kevin's words and all the other research I had conducted, I was expecting something significant to happen on my walk-through, even in the daytime. But as we strolled around I felt nothing, and even Joanne didn't feel much other than several areas of intense cold. Frankly, I was a little disappointed. That's when I contacted Rich.

KPI is a no-nonsense organization and has been designated as a Family Member of The Atlantic Paranormal Society (TAPS), because they have demonstrated to TAPS that they are professional, experienced, and knowledgeable. Upon hearing my request, Rich was only too happy to give us a personal tour through the cemetery at night when paranormal activity was greatest. And since KPI uses Page Jackson to train new investigators who join the group, conducting training sessions at least twice a year, Rich knows the cemetery well.

Following Rich off the highway, we drove another hundred yards or so down a sandy road into Page Jackson and pulled off into a cleared area. We got out of our vehicles. Since KPI had been in the area so often, Rich had already drawn up a map that divided the cemetery into sectors to be investigated. During training he would pair up his investigators, an experienced investigator with a new one, and would issue the equipment each individual wanted to use: EMF detectors, digital cameras, thermal sensors, and the like. Everyone was free to choose whatever equipment they wished or none at all, but everyone had to carry at least a flashlight and a two-way radio.

Because Rich had arranged this investigation for our benefit, he and Kim took charge of us and didn't plan to restrict our movements to any particular sector. He was going to guide us

Page Jackson Cemetery is home to several ghosts who make their presence known at night.

through the entire cemetery and even into the Shiloh Cemetery adjacent to Page Jackson, if time permitted. Because we were going to stay together, we carried only flashlights, cameras, and voice recorders. Rich gave us a few final words about safety and led us off into the brush. With some apprehension, I flicked on my light and followed, heading east along a sandy trail. Kim was in the lead. Only a few yards down the trail, she stopped and motioned for us to be silent. We heard rustling in the bushes nearby. Then we heard whistling, a quiet, happy little tune. Kim smiled, "It's Neal. He's behind that tree over there," and pointed to a nearby oak.

Neal had revealed himself to Kim several years before and has developed a relationship with her and with several other paranormal investigators. Kim first met him near a dirt mound not far away on the north side of the cemetery. She was walking down the adjacent road when a large black shadow passed in front of her, and then a small, barefoot, Tom Sawyer-like boy came streaking across. He ran behind a clump of trees and disappeared.

Rich and Kim haven't been able to learn anything about the boy's background, but Kim has talked to him several times, and he seems to be very friendly. I would have been a bit skeptical about this "sighting," except for the rustling bushes and whistling. The foliage in that area wasn't so dense that I would not have seen someone. And later in talking to the other investigators, especially the sensitive ones, I learned that they all had had experiences with Neal.

We moved on to the east, walking quietly and slowly. I was leading, when suddenly I walked into an icy pocket of air. This wasn't Florida-after-the-heat-of-the-day cool. This was upper Midwest-February-night frigid. It was icy cold. I came to an abrupt halt and backed up a few steps, bumping into Rich. I turned to apologize, but he just put his finger to his lips, signaling me to keep silent. Kim was in the rear talking quietly to someone. She explained it was her friend, Annie, who inhabited that section of Page Jackson.

Kim related that Annie had been a young girl in her late teens attending a picnic in a green field nearby in 1911. She remembered being happy and even singing a little song, when something happened and she suddenly found herself in the cemetery. She doesn't remember how she died, but she thinks it had something to do with the picnic. Kim described her as a pretty, petite, red-haired girl. She still sang her little song occasionally.

Kim was the only one who could hear what Annie was saying, but the gist of the conversation was, first, who were these new people? Kim told her who we were and that I was writing a book about the cemetery. She seemed satisfied with that. And, second, she warned Kim quite sternly that we should turn around and not continue down the road. When Kim asked why,

Annie wouldn't give her a reason. She just told us to turn around and go back the way we had come. Then she disappeared.

We discussed Annie's warning for a few moments and finally decided to heed her advice. We turned and headed back to the west. Seconds later, we heard five or six shots from a handgun rather close by. Someone in the houses beside the cemetery obviously was doing the shooting. We had no idea whether the shots were being fired randomly into the woods or at another person, but we all were thankful for Annie's warning. A coincidence? I didn't know, but coincidence or not, it was timely.

We meandered through the rest of the cemetery and down into Shiloh without any more encounters, while Rich and Kim regaled us with their many paranormal experiences in the cemetery. Once Kim and another investigator were on the main road that runs through Page Jackson and heard horse's hooves galloping toward them. They shined their lights in the direction of the noise but saw nothing. The sounds continued straight toward them, and the two investigators jumped out of the way as the phantom horse ran right by. When Kim examined the area, there were no hoof-prints of any kind in the sand.

Both Kim and Rich have captured paranormal voices on tape, not only Neal's whistling and Annie's singing, but other unidentified voices. "Look at me." "Back again." "You're stupid." They both also have been touched and have seen many black masses crossing the road and moving through the brush. Kim has also seen a Bigfoot-sized being crossing the road.

And there is Nathan Bowers. When KPI first started coming to Page Jackson, Lois Lee, a medium and one of the investigators who has since gone on to form her own group, caught glimpses of a tall, broad-shouldered man wearing a plaid shirt and overalls. He was wild-eyed and talking to himself, obviously very angry about something. But over the years he has mellowed and has had several conversations with Kim. He has identified himself as Nathan Bowers, a lifelong resident of Sanford, and has said he loved to fish. He has asked Kim to tell his mother he is okay, a request Kim is unable to fulfill—Nathan died over a hundred years ago.

Standing in the cool evening air in the Shiloh Cemetery, Rich and Kim finally exhausted their stories, and it was time to head home. We walked slowly back up the sandy trail to our cars, put away our equipment, and said goodnight to each other. As I got into my truck and drove off, I mentally said goodnight to the several ghosts of Page Jackson Cemetery.

Spotlight on Lake Mary

Most people don't realize that Florida was as wild and wooly as the West ever was. Cattle ranged freely without any fences until the 1930s, and almost everyone had a horse. A lady named Harriet Mixon owned the land where the Lake Mary City Hall now stands. She also owned a little dapple-gray Cracker horse named Shorty and pastured him in a paddock on her land across the street from the Lake Mary Tavern.

Shorty was a smart horse. Not long after Harriet Mixon bought him, he learned how to unlatch the gate to his small pasture and get out. And not long after that, he started going across the road, into the tavern, and up to the bar. After a few such outings, the bartender, as a joke, filled a small bucket with beer and set it on the bar for Shorty, who quickly drank it down, belched, and sauntered back out of the bar, none the worse for wear. Shorty's sojourn to the Lake Mary Tavern became a habit. It didn't seem to harm the horse, and his visits were great for business. This went on for several years until Shorty finally died, a contented horse who had lived a good life. Harriet Mixon, who herself was a frequent visitor to the tavern, and the many patrons held a fitting funeral for Shorty and buried him in his pasture across the road in sight of the bar. They figured if Shorty could see his favorite haunt, he would be as happy in death as he was in life.

A week after Shorty's funeral, the bartender on a rather slow evening was astonished to hear the clip-clop, clip-clop of a horse. The door opened wide by itself and the clip-clops approached the bar. Then they stopped, and the bartender could hear breathing and a whiny. Shorty was back. Neither the bartender nor any of the patrons could see Shorty, but they could hear him and almost feel him. Shorty wanted his beer. So the barkeep dutifully filled his bucket and set it on the bar. For several years after that, Shorty's ghost came to the tavern once or twice a week.

Old timers in Lake Mary all swear this is true, although no one can say exactly when these events occurred. No matter what—the ghostly appearances of Shorty, the beer-drinking horse, make a good story.

CHAPTER 19

Pinewood Cemetery
DAYTONA BEACH

DAYTONA BEACH IS AS FLAT AS A PANCAKE—
except for one small, man-made hill where the Pinewood Cemetery now stands across Main Street from the aptly named Boot Hill Saloon. James W. Smith purchased the four-and-a-half acres of what was to become the Pinewood Cemetery and the land around it in 1853 and homesteaded it. He and his wife had a child, a girl, named Alena Beatrice. She was an only child and was her father's pride and joy. He wanted only the best for his baby girl, so he decided to set aside the four-and-a-half acres as a gift to his daughter when she wed. He called the property "Momento."

Some say that when Alena was in her teens and starting to think of marriage, she decided that Momento was too flat; she couldn't see the ocean from there. Daddy's darling's wish was his command, and he brought in fill dirt to raise the area high enough to see the ocean. Others say he did so to alleviate drainage problems. Whatever the reason, Momento became a hill.

As she grew into womanhood, Alena often walked around Momento, imagining her wedding and the house she and her husband would build. She even planned her wedding on the grounds. She was a beautiful young woman and had many suitors, but, alas, her dreams went unfulfilled. In April 1877, she contracted smallpox and passed away on April 15. Alena was laid to rest on her hill in a white batiste wedding gown. She was the first person to be buried in what then became known as the Smith Family Burial Grounds and later Pinewood Cemetery.

In the early 1900s, after Mr. Smith and his wife died, Charles Bingham and Jerome Maley took over the cemetery and formed the Pinewood Cemetery Corporation, which maintained it until the Great Depression wiped out the company. For many years Pinewood lay uncared for and vandalized, until local interests finally provided the funds to preserve this beautiful and historic burial ground.

And Pinewood is a beautiful cemetery. Because it is on a small hill, there is very little flat area for graves, so through the years it has been terraced with bright, white stone walls. In the daytime, it fairly glows, with the gleaming white terraces set off even more by green grass, pine and live oak trees, and the wrought iron fence which surrounds it.

I first came across the Pinewood Cemetery in a fascinating little book, *Haunted Daytona Beach*, by Dusty Smith and published by The History Press (2007). I was intrigued by the story and called the author, who with both a scientific bent and psychic abilities, heads the Daytona Beach Paranormal Research Group and Haunts of the World's Most Famous Beach Ghost Tours.

Sue and I met Dusty for a tour one brisk January evening at the corner of Peninsula and Main, across from the cemetery, which, by the way, is considered the fourth most paranormally active in Florida. She likes to keep her tour groups small and intimate, so there were only six of us, and I must say that the hour or so that we were together was fascinating.

According to Dusty, Alena Smith (no relation to Dusty) loved her little sanctuary more than people thought. She's still there. Sightings of Alena began in the 1920s and have continued ever since. On April 15, the anniversary of her death, many locals claim to see a beautiful young woman in a long, white, batiste gown wandering the grounds of Pinewood. She is the most seen and photographed entity in the cemetery.

Then, there is the story of Bonnie and Slim. Bonnie was a barmaid at the Brass Rail Saloon, down the street from the Pinewood Cemetery. She was a tiny woman, not quite five feet tall, and carried a barstool around with her to gain a little elevation. Slim was a giant, almost seven feet, and worked at the livery stables nearby. In the evenings, Slim liked to relax with a beer and took to hanging out in the Brass Rail. The first time he saw Bonnie, he was smitten and went there every night. He was a shy and quiet man and found it hard to express his love for her. Finally, though, Bonnie got the picture and helped Slim along with a little flirting. After many months, they became a couple.

Slim lived in a room at the stables and had an old, broken-down horse, which wasn't much good for anything. But it suited Slim just fine. It got him around town when he needed transportation, and it allowed him to escort Bonnie home after she finished work. They were a sight, the two of them on the old horse, plodding down Main Street, Slim, his feet almost dragging the ground, little Bonnie perched like a queen behind him, toting her barstool.

A beautiful cemetery, with pine and live oak trees, Pinewood is still a haunted place, with ghosts like Slim and Bonnie, the doomed lovers.

A couple of years passed, and their love deepened. Slim knew he wanted to spend the rest of his life with Bonnie and began diligently saving his money so that they could marry. Finally, one evening Slim plucked up his courage with the help of several beers. While they were plodding along to Bonnie's house after the bar closed, he asked her to be his wife. Bonnie was delirious with happiness. Slim, too, in his somewhat less than sober state, was overjoyed and proud of himself for getting up the nerve to propose.

On the way home from Bonnie's, Slim was thinking how wonderful it was going to be spending his nights and days with his love. He should have been paying attention to the road. His horse trotted under a tree, and a branch knocked Slim off, breaking his neck.

The undertaker notified Bonnie the following morning. She was devastated and could not be consoled. They buried Slim on the east side of Pinewood two days later. For three months, Bonnie visited Slim's grave every day, morning and night. Then one day she didn't show up for work at the Brass Rail, and her boss went to look for her. He found her hanging in her house, her barstool lying on the floor beneath her. And she did leave a note. In it she asked that her barstool be placed in her coffin—there was plenty of room, because she was so small—and that she be buried next to Slim.

Slim and Bonnie are still seen in Pinewood to this day, a giant of a man and the tiny wisp of a woman. In addition to the sightings, photos and videos have been made of the ghostly lovers.

Paranormally, the most active section of the cemetery is the McCoy area. Bill McCoy loved boats. In the early 1900s he and his brother, Ben, built luxury vessels for many people, including the Vanderbilts and the Wannamakers. Of course, they built their own boat in 1903, the *Uncle Sam,* which they used for day trips in the local area. By 1920, however, boats were out of fashion, and the McCoy boys began looking for something else to do. They desperately wanted to continue earning their living on the water.

In January 1920, the Eighteenth Amendment to the U. S. Constitution went into effect, and alcohol became illegal throughout America—Prohibition had arrived. Rum-running quickly became popular. At first, authorities were lax in enforcement of the law. By 1925, there were estimates of thirty thousand to one-hundred thousand speakeasies in New York City alone. So Bill purchased the ninety-foot *Henry Marshall,* which could carry fifteen hundred cases of booze, and docked it in the Bahamas. His first run successfully delivered a huge cargo of liquor to New York, and he became known as the "King of Rum Row." With the money he earned from that run, he purchased the much larger, faster *Arethusa* and boasted in later years that during his rum-running days he had delivered 170,000 cases.

Unlike many of the rum-runners who watered down their liquor to increase profits, Bill refused. Soon he earned a reputation for "honesty," and the phrase, "Is that the real McCoy?" is still with us to this day.

As Prohibition continued, the government increased its enforcement efforts, and Bill was often under surveillance by revenue agents. But Bill was clever. When he thought the revenuers were on to him, he changed the registry of his vessel and its name. Under Bahamian registry, the ship was named the *Tomoka,* and under the French he called it the *Marie Celeste.* Finally, the Coast Guard cutter *Seneca* went after him and took him under fire. Bill surrendered, ending his days as a rumrunner.

He died in 1948 and is buried along with his brother in Pinewood Cemetery. In life Bill and Ben were pretty wild and liked to party. That must be why locals still smell cigarette smoke and hear drunken laughter, breaking glass, and old tavern songs coming from the McCoy section of the cemetery.

Some of the guests on our tour took photos and captured many orbs, especially in the McCoy area. Some even heard the little boy, Stephen, clacking his stick along the fence on the north side of the cemetery, but that's another story. You'll have to take Dusty's tour to hear it.

Spotlight on Ponce Inlet Lighthouse

The Ponce de León Inlet Lighthouse, as it is officially known, has been around for a long time. The original lighthouse was built on the south side of Mosquito Inlet in 1835, but the oil for the lamp was never delivered, and Indian attacks in the Second Seminole War all but destroyed the tower. The area was then abandoned.

Eventually, after many shipwrecks near the Mosquito Inlet, a lighthouse was finally erected and put into operation in 1887. At the south end of Daytona Beach, the Ponce Inlet Lighthouse was not bad duty. Still, the original kerosene lamp needed constant attention as did the later incandescent oil vapor lamp, and the light keeper had little free time.

Even though the lighthouse was near Daytona, living at the Ponce Inlet Lighthouse was relatively isolated, and the keepers and their families were often lonely. Although there were few suicides and infirmities associated with isolation at the lighthouse, those who lived there had their problems.

The lighthouse itself doesn't seem to be haunted, at least not according to my ghost ferret, Joanne, but the keepers' quarters brim with paranormal activity. There are three keeper's houses. One is glassed off for viewing only, which, according to Joanne, is a pity, because it is "full of feeling." She is desperate to get in the house and check it out.

The remaining two houses, on the other hand, are open to the public and are full of spirits. One has the strong presence of a woman, probably a keeper's wife or perhaps one of the female keepers. Joanne thinks the room, which now houses uniforms, was her bedroom.

The third house is also glassed off, but there is on display a weird-looking china doll, something like the doll in the Audubon

House in Key West. It immediately caught Joanne's attention. She started taking digital photographs at an angle so she wouldn't get any reflection. She took several pictures and when she looked at them, there was an orb. It moved around in each frame. She took more pictures. The orb seemed to have a mind of its own. Finally, she decided she'd experienced enough and left the house.

But as she departed, a feeling came over her, as though something had attached itself to her. She went to the restroom and the feeling still clung to her. "Get off me," she demanded in a loud, angry voice. Several women in the restroom stared at her, but the feeling left.

Someday Joanne hopes to get into all of the keepers' houses and do a real walk-through. She'd like to find out exactly what had been clinging to her. As for me, I'll wait for her at the bar down the road on the Inlet.

North

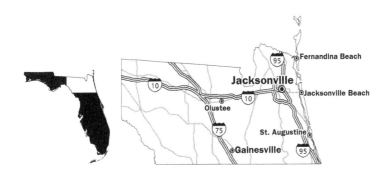

Fernandina Beach
  The Amelia Island Williams House

Jacksonville Beach
  Homestead Restaurant

Olustee
  Olustee Battlefield Historic State Park

St. Augustine
  Ripley's Believe It or Not! Museum
  Spanish Military Hospital

CHAPTER 20

The Spanish Military Hospital Museum

ST. AUGUSTINE

HUMAN BONES WERE DISCOVERED on the approximate site of the Spanish Military Hospital on Avilés Street, just south of the Plaza in St. Augustine. Apparently, it was the cemetery of the first Catholic church built in the 1580s by the Spanish, about where the A1A Ale Works now sits in this, the oldest city in America. It may also have been an Indian burial ground for thousands of years before Admiral Pedro Menendez de Avilés landed there on September 6, 1565.

St. Augustine, now 445 years old, exudes an Old World atmosphere and has a mystical aura about it, even though it is often overrun by tourists. Numerous hurricanes, epidemics, and warfare have all left their mark. The town was also ransacked and burned by the British on several occasions. But each time, after each disaster, St. Augustinians buried their dead, rebuilt their city, and carried on.

The original Spanish Military Hospital was built in 1793 near the bay where it could catch the fresh sea breezes. It served variously as a hospital and as a livery stable until 1821, when the United States took possession of Florida. The building there now is an exact replica and built on the foundations of the original. It was erected in 1967 and serves as a museum, giving us a glimpse of hospital life during the late 1700s.

The main rooms include a ward room where the sick and injured were housed, a surgeon's office containing equipment used by eighteenth-century physicians, an apothecary with various medicines and herbs, and a mourning room where the dying were taken to separate them from the other patients in the ward room. There is also an attic or loft where attendants might have been housed or hay stored when the building was a livery. Women were allowed only in the mourning room to be with dying relatives.

Sue and I visited the Spanish Military Hospital Museum many years ago when I was working on *Ghosts of St. Augustine*. I don't believe that any paranormal investigations of the building had been done at that time, but the docent who escorted us through the Museum complained of several incidents where guests had been touched and even bitten on the ankles. Still, there didn't seem to be enough to warrant a good story—this was before I met Joanne, my sensitive friend, and I knew no other sensitives—so I didn't include it in that first book. Since then the Museum staff has experienced a great deal of activity, and numerous investigators have studied the place.

Thanks to my friends at Peace River Ghost Tracker, I was able to get an interview with Diane Lane and Susan Harrell of Ancient City Tours, which now manages the Museum. We met Diane on a cold January day, fittingly overcast and gloomy, and she led us up to their offices in what once was the attic.

Diane and Susan began regaling us with the history and many stories of the place. One morning a woman from Orlando walked in. Susan was at the counter. "This is going to sound strange," the woman said, "but do you have any rubber stamps in here?"

Susan thought she wanted to buy some. "No, but there's a store just down the street."

"No. That's not what I meant. I was on your tour last night and silently asked, 'Is anyone here?' I felt kind of foolish saying it out loud. Anyway, this morning when I got up, I looked in the mirror and saw 'yes' on my back. I was freaked out and was wondering if you might have stamps in here and someone somehow had stamped my back," and she raised the back of her shirt to show Susan.

Susan said that incident made everyone on the staff realize something paranormal was definitely going on in the Museum.

Once Candy and Diane were sitting at their adjacent desks. They both looked up and saw a man ascending the stairs. When he reached the top landing, he evaporated. Wide-eyed, Diane asked, "Did you see that?" Candy nodded, "Yeah, I did." They both shook their heads and went back to their work.

Diane told the story of a high school science club that had come to the Museum for an evening tour. They were sitting on benches in the ward room. Their teacher was seated alone off to the side. The kids were getting restless when suddenly a strand of the teacher's hair on the left side of her face raised up in the air for a few seconds and then fell. Moments later a strand of her hair rose on the right side, was suspended for some sec-

The beds in the Spanish Military Hospital have been known to move on their own.

onds, and fell. The kids, awe-struck, stared at her, and the room became deathly still. Finally, the teacher gathered her wits and said, "Okay. We came, we saw, and we're leaving." And the whole group scrambled for the door.

Susan remembered an incident that occurred during the daytime with a paranormal investigator, who was talking to Susan and several others at the front counter. A heavy, iron garden staff, which was put outside at night with a lantern hanging from it, stood propped in a far corner. Without warning the staff flew directly at the investigator. Susan screamed, and jumped over the counter out of the way. The staff clanged to the floor.

Susan related that one of the tour guides, Joe Clemson, had a group of almost forty people in the ward room. Suddenly she heard a commotion and opened the door to see some forty people rushing for the exit, all trying to get out at the same time. Once outside, she asked Joe what had happened.

"Gee, I don't know," he replied. "The beds started moving around and bumping people on their legs. Some guy looked at me and said, 'Joe, this isn't funny," and I told him, 'I'm not doing that.' Then a bed smacked into somebody and we were out of there!"

Susan had another experience with the beds. She is an extremely neat and tidy person—everything in its place. One morning she opened the Museum to find the beds in the ward room askew and a very old crucifix, which had hung on the wall, lying on the floor. She rushed upstairs ready to ring the neck of the tour guide who had left the mess the night before. She was especially angry about the crucifix, because it was an antique dating from the First Spanish Period.

Diane was already in the office. "What are you ranting about?"

Susan snapped back, "Have you seen the mess downstairs, the beds all over the place and the crucifix on the floor? Who had the tour last night?"

Calmly, Diane replied, "Susan, there was no tour last night. No one was in the building after we closed."

Without another word Susan went back downstairs, straightened the beds, and put the crucifix in a safer place.

Opening the Museum in the morning, the staff often finds the brochures in the rack by the counter strewn over the floor. Tour guides on the evening tours hear footsteps upstairs when no one is there. People get touched and hear moaning in the mourning room. Human shadows move across the walls when no one else is around. Once a TAPS team was investigating the Museum and requested that the electricity be turned off and all electrical equipment unplugged. A short time later, the unplugged printer upstairs inexplicably started spewing out paper.

Peace River Ghost Tracker has also investigated the Museum. One evening Scott and Sprout, along with Chris and Lucas, two guides from Ancient City Tours, were standing outside taking a break. Scott decided to go back in and change tapes in a recorder. He rushed out seconds later. He said he had a sweet taste in his mouth, and both his mouth and lips were becoming numb.

Chris thought for a moment. "That sounds like clove oil. They used to use that stuff for dental work. Let's go take a look."

Everyone went inside to the apothecary. Chris studied the room then picked up a bottle from one of the tables. It contained clove oil. Chris and Lucas also noticed that it appeared the bottles and containers on the table had been rearranged. They had taken photos of all the rooms at the beginning of the investigation, and when they compared the table with their pictures, they found that the bottles had indeed been moved.

On a previous investigation Scott had gone into the mourning room and gently laid down on the bed. He had laid there for some time trying to think how a dying soldier might behave, what he might say. Then he had begun talking, reenacting the part of a dying soldier. Sprout was just outside and described Scott's voice as heartbreaking. He said things such as "Help me. Hold my hand. Are you there?" As he continued speaking, something, or someone, firmly grabbed his hand. At that, Scott sat up, thanked the spirit, and left the room.

On this occasion, he attempted to recreate what had happened to him before. As he lay down and started speaking, his EMF meter as well as the recorder set up in the doorway to capture audio began spiking, and he got an EVP which sounded like "sitting here" with an English accent.

There is no doubt that this place is haunted. As Sue and I stood at the door saying our goodbyes to Diane and Susan, we all agreed that many of the entities now residing in the Museum were brought there as patients and never left. And as we stepped out of the cozy building and into the mist and gloom, I thought the Spanish Military Hospital wasn't a bad place to be.

CHAPTER 21

Ripley's Believe It Or Not! Museum

ST. AUGUSTINE

RIPLEY'S BELIEVE IT OR NOT! MUSEUM in St. Augustine has always fascinated me. I have been there many times, and even though I had written about it for one of my previous books, I decided to take a fresh look at this remarkable place in *Ghosthunting Florida*.

In researching that first story, Joanne, my intrepid, sensitive friend, and I visited a couple of times and actually conducted an investigation with members of the Ripley's staff and Sandy Craig, owner of A Ghostly Experience Tours. During that session, Joanne empathetically experienced the suffocation and death of a female by smoke inhalation. She also felt that this female ghost was trying to keep her out of the area to save her. We later discovered that two women actually had died there in the 1940s, the result of smoke inhalation from a fire.

The structure was built in 1887 by William Warden, a friend of Henry Flagler and John D. Rockefeller. He named it "Castle Warden," and it was the family winter home until 1925. It then sat empty for sixteen years. In 1941, Marjorie Kinnan Rawlings, Pulitzer Prize-winning author of *The Yearling*, and her husband purchased the mansion and turned it into the Castle Warden Hotel.

In April 1944 a fire erupted, perhaps caused by a dropped cigarette, and two women, Ruth Pickering and Betty Richeson, a young socialite from Jacksonville, died. Although the fire was contained on the top two floors, and the damage was not extensive, Marjorie Rawlings and her husband had lost their enthusiasm for the place and put it up for sale.

Robert Ripley, the famous collector, had been a frequent visitor and, in fact, had tried to purchase Castle Warden several times. He had wanted to use it as an "odditorium" to house his collection of weird curios. Unfortunately, he died in May 1949, but his heirs obtained the mansion a few months later. In 1950, Castle Warden became the first Ripley's Believe It Or Not! Museum.

There is no record of paranormal activity during the time when "The Castle" was the Warden home, but it certainly became known for its ghostly bent after it opened as the Ripley Museum. And no wonder. With hundreds of oddities from around the world, including shrunken heads, Voodoo dolls, ancient weapons of all types, witch doctors' masks, and the like, it is no surprise that there might be entities and energy attached to many of the artifacts.

When I decided to include Ripley's in this collection for America's Haunted Road Trip, I contacted Susan Harrell, who had worked there from 2006 to 2009 as the Director of Ghost Adventures; Ralf Ingwersen, the present Ghost Tours Director; Diane Lane, owner of Ancient City Tours, which now runs the tours for Ripley's; and my friends from Peace River Ghost Tracker, Scott Walker and Sprout Dvorak. All have had paranormal experiences in the Museum.

Sue and I first went to visit Susan and Diane. They had some great stories. Susan told me about the new general manager who had arrived in 2006. He was a hands-on person and attended many of the tour rehearsals, which Ripley's requires of their storytellers. As he followed the rehearsal into the Circus Room on the second floor, someone yanked his hair from behind. Furious, he turned around to confront a young employee behind him. The young man backed away surprised, assuring his boss that he would never, ever do anything like that. Could it have been done by an entity that cowers in a nearby corner? No one ever found out, but the general manager was always careful in that room. He never had his hair pulled again, but he often felt pressure on his shoulders when passing through.

Susan had her own "hair-raising" experience near the exit. In preparation for an evening tour, she was pulling curtains in place, both arms raised, when someone started running fingers through her hair. She spun around and shouted at her coworker, Dave, who had been teasing her earlier about her new, very short haircut. She stopped suddenly. Dave was not there. Neither was anyone else. She was alone. With that realization, she ran from the room and back to the safety of her office.

In the evenings, Ripley's runs a Ghost Train, which tours the city and ends at the Museum, where the guests are treated to a tour through the building. About thirty minutes before the train arrives, an employee unlocks all the doors. That was what Rachel was doing when she realized she had misplaced her two-way radio. Since she was already up on the third floor, she called Susan on a house phone and asked if she'd bring another radio upstairs. Susan was very uncomfortable going up the stairs after dark, so she asked Dave to go with her. Halfway up to the second floor, they both sensed someone following them. It was not a pleasant feeling. They ran up to the second floor. The door was locked. Frightened now, they raced up to the third floor, the thing pursuing them close behind. Susan lunged for the door but found it also locked. Dave stood between the stairs and Susan, protecting her, while she fumbled for her keys and unlocked the door. They finally burst into the Bone Room and found Rachel. When they breathlessly told her what had just happened, she was amazed. "I unlocked every door on the way up."

Susan and the other employees had many experiences in the Museum, most of them pleasant and all of them exciting, but probably the most bizarre was what happened to one of Susan's storytellers, Brenda*, now retired. She was always uneasy in the Theater Room; there seemed to be a very unpleasant spirit there. Perhaps the same one who had pulled the general manager's hair. Brenda often found it difficult to complete a thought, let alone a whole story. As weeks passed, she became more and more uncomfortable in the room. This culminated in one frightening event. She had a tour group in the theater and was in mid-sentence, when unseen hands gripped her throat. She stood paralyzed for what seemed like an eternity, unable to speak. Finally, when she did find her voice, she could say only a few phrases—and in French! Brenda quickly ushered her group out of the theater and was again able to speak normally. She completed the tour, but "retired" immediately after she finished.

Ralf Ingwersen, the present Ghost Tours Director, reports that the inexplicable activity continues. Recently Roberta, one of the managers, was in the lobby at closing time and heard a woman crying and moaning. No one else was present. Later that evening she was talking to one of the ticket sellers, who told her she had had a "weird" experience earlier in the day. "I heard what sounded like a woman whimpering in the lobby. I looked around, and no one was there. It happened twice."

That same evening before locking up, Roberta toured the building to make sure no visitors remained. In the Theater Room, she saw a strange light in the right rear corner. At first she thought it might be a dehumidifier that had shorted out and was sparking, but the light was not like a lightning flash. It was more of a hazy glow like reflected moonlight. It rose several feet in the air and then disappeared. There are no windows in the Theater Room.

Ralf had his own experience. There was to be a night launch of the Space Shuttle from Cape Canaveral a few miles south. He wanted to see it, so he went up to the fourth-floor penthouse for a good view. As he stepped into the room to get out on the roof, he was overcome by crushing despair and sadness, a heavy feeling weighing him down with grief and gloom. It stunned him, and he stood there trying to understand what had brought it on. Suddenly he realized that this was the room in which Ruth Pickering had died during the 1944 fire.

Scott and Sprout from PRGT always nod in agreement when they hear others' stories about Ripley's. They and their team have had many experiences of their own during three investigations there.

On one of their earlier investigations, Scott was sitting on the landing between the second and third floors where a moose head is hanging. He began conducting an EVP session. Suddenly something surrounded him, and his heart felt as if it were pounding out of his chest. He stood and walked up to the Bone Room on the next floor. There Craig was experiencing the same sensations. At that point, Scott called everyone outside for a break.

After the team returned to the building, Toni and Scott returned to the moose head, and she began feeling dizzy and nauseous and seeing shadows moving around her. During a later investigation, the whole PRGT team and Ralf went back to the moose head, and Toni and Sprout again became nauseous and disoriented, seeing red and yellow streaks of light on the ceiling.

During my visits to the Museum, I've never heard, seen, or felt anything, but I have always been enthralled by the experiences others have had there. Maybe the next time I return, someone—or something—will run fingers through my hair. Or I'll smell smoke from a long-ago fire.

Spotlight on Wellborn

North Florida can be a pretty spooky place. Dozens of tiny, old towns dot the landscape in an otherwise lightly developed area: Monticello, McAlpin, Bramford, White Springs, all of these peopled by hard working generations of Cracker families who have lived and died close to the land, many buried in long-forgotten, overgrown cemeteries adjacent to abandon farmhouses. Wellborn, near the intersection of I-10 and I-75, population 2,600, is one of these towns.

A few years ago a young woman who lived in Wellborn was exploring the back roads just to the west of town, when she came across what she thought might have been a cemetery. She pulled off the road and got out of her car to take a look. Sadness overcame her as she wandered through the weeds, stopping to look at the tombstones that were still legible. Many weren't. Most of the graves were of children less than twelve years of age. The last burial she could determine occurred in 1864. How sad that this sacred place was so neglected.

She walked through the graveyard for several more minutes, then started back out to the road when she heard leaves rustling behind her. She turned abruptly and saw a misty gray form floating through the trees at the back of the cemetery. At first petrified, she gathered her senses and raced back to her car.

She talked her husband into going back the following day. With him by her side, she wasn't frightened as she had been the day before, so they walked throughout the cemetery and behind it. There, outside the rusted, broken-down fence, she saw a half-rotted wooden grave marker, an oak having grown partially around it. The name and date of death, if they had ever been inscribed, were no longer visible, and she had to look carefully even to know it was a grave marker. She had no idea why the grave was outside the cemetery. A slave? A suicide? A criminal? An adulterer? No one would ever know.

And what about the apparition she'd seen the day before? Had she imagined it? She would probably never know that either.

Still, cemeteries are great places to explore, whether for hunting ghosts or just searching interesting gravestones. And with all the small family and churchyard graves around, North Florida is a great place to do it.

CHAPTER 22

Homestead Restaurant
JACKSONVILLE BEACH

I LOVE FRIED CHICKEN! I can't remember a time in my life when fried chicken wasn't my favorite food. My mother made the best I'd ever tasted—until I met Sue. Hers is even better—really. She doesn't prepare it anymore because it provides such generous amounts of cholesterol and also because the frying splatters grease everywhere, so when friends tell me of a great fried chicken restaurant, I sneak out and get a fix.

That's what happened with the Homestead Restaurant in Jacksonville Beach. My friend Greg lives in Jacksonville and was aware of my passion for fried chicken. He also knew that I was working on this book. He called one day. "Hey, buddy. I have found the ultimate fried chicken restaurant." He paused. "And, it's haunted."

I almost jumped out of my chair. He told me a little about the Homestead, and I started to salivate. As he talked, the wheels began turning in my head. "Jax Beach" was two-and-a-half hours from my house, and it is open only for dinner, except on Sundays. This was not going to be a stealth operation. I was going to have to sweet talk my wife. Fortunately, Sue, a thoroughly Southern lady, has her weaknesses: fried okra, collard greens, and fried green tomatoes. "Well, just this once, but you're eating salads the rest of the week," she told me. So, once again, we headed up I-95 for a bit of manna.

You can't tell it from the outside because of the siding, but the Homestead is actually a log cabin, rustic but cozy inside. The pine log cabin was built as a private residence in 1932. When the owner died two years later, he left it to Alpha Paynter. She at first opened a boarding house, which was popular during the years of the Great Depression. But by 1947, boarding houses were no longer in vogue, so she converted it into a restaurant. Alpha Paynter must have learned to fry chicken from my mother, because even then the Homestead's fried chicken was famous. After fifteen years, Paynter's health began to fail, and she sold the restaurant to Preben and Nina Johansen. Sadly, Alpha Paynter died in December of the same year. Legend says that she was buried in the woods behind the restaurant, and that may be true, but records indicate that she was cremated. So perhaps her ashes were buried or scattered there.

The Homestead went through a succession of owners, including Kathy Marvin, the daughter of the Johansens, and her husband, and it continued to be famous for its chicken. However, after a lengthy road construction project along Beach Boulevard in front of the restaurant, the owners were forced to close. In 2008, Abbas and Judy Bagheri reopened the Homestead, and it has quickly regained its homey and comfortable reputation, although chicken and dumplings has now become the most famous dish on the menu.

We arrived early, the place not yet crowded, and ordered drinks while we looked over the menu, although I knew exactly what I wanted to eat. While we waited, Greg began to tell us all he knew about the ghosts and paranormal activity in the restaurant.

Alpha Paynter is probably the entity most often experienced in the Homestead. The big, old fireplace that she used to heat the building is still there near the front door. In life, she often sat rocking before it during the winter, a toasty fire burning on the hearth. When she ran the boarding house and the weather was bad, she would sit in her rocker, reading by the fire light, waiting for all her boarders to return safely. Now, she is often seen by staff and patrons, standing in front of the fire, staring into it.

Some employees have seen an elderly woman in a long dress walking up the stairs to the office and storage room. Since no one is allowed in that area except the staff, they have run after her to tell her she is not supposed to go there. But when they have gotten near the spot where they saw her, she has disappeared.

There is also the disturbing legend of Angle Rosenburg and her daughter, Annie. Legend says that right after the Civil War, a woman named Angle Rosenburg ran some sort of adoption agency in the cabin that is now the Homestead Restaurant. Since it is a verified fact that the cabin was built in 1932, perhaps the cabin built then might have included an older structure existing from the Civil War, or another building may have occupied the site. We do know that, according to local archives, Angle Rosenburg did exist. However, I could find no record of Annie Rosenburg, who apparently worked with abandoned and orphaned children. She herself may also have been a widow, her husband killed in the Civil War. In any case, she was a sad, forlorn woman, probably what we would term clinically depressed. The oral tradition is that Angle Rosenburg hanged herself in a back room, and her daughter, Annie, did the same ten years later upstairs in a storage area.

No one knows if the story is true, but several people have had experiences with female apparitions. One young woman went into the ladies room, and while she was washing her hands, she looked into the mirror and saw an older woman standing behind her, staring at her. Unnerved, the girl turned around. No one else was in the room. She turned back to finish rinsing and drying her hands, and she saw the woman again. This time she realized that she was probably seeing a ghost. She froze. As she stood there unable to move, the woman said, "Enjoy what you do and take care of those around you." Then she vanished. The girl screamed and raced out of the restroom. Whether this apparition was Angle Rosenburg or Alpha Paynter, no one will ever know.

Annie Rosenburg, or someone believed to be Annie, also has been seen upstairs sitting in a chair in a storage room and look-ing out the back window. She is a young woman, perhaps eigh-teen or nineteen, and is wearing a dark dress. She looks very sad. Those who have seen her say they've also heard children playing outside. Is she watching over some of the orphans? Is it really Annie? Or is it perhaps someone's wild imagination triggered by stories about Annie?

There are many other stories about the Homestead. Greg said that he was in the men's room once and all the faucets came on full blast. When he walked over to turn them off, they all shut off by themselves. Our waiter told us that he had gone into the restroom once himself, and all the doors locked on their own. He just said in a stern voice, "Okay, knock it off. I've got custom-ers waiting." The doors unlocked and opened—all of them.

There are other little occurrences. Lights turn on and off when no one is near the switches. That happens fairly often after closing as the staff is trying to clean up and go home. Pots, pans, and utensils in the kitchen get moved about overnight. A woman can be heard humming in several locations in the restaurant. The sound of wine bottles clinking together can also be heard. Plates inside cabinets break on their own. Candles light by themselves. But these are all minor incidents that only tend to add atmosphere to the Homestead. Employees love the place and are quite comfortable there.

I listened to Greg and took a lot of notes, but it was good that Sue was along. She was taking notes too, and she hadn't buried her face in fried chicken. When we finally finished dinner and our lengthy conversation, I was groaning from eating so much. I didn't even have room for the peach cobbler. No matter. I'd just had one of the best meals of my life—and a great story. I was already thinking about arranging to join Greg—to go "fishing." That's one thing Sue doesn't like to do, so I'm sure she'll stay home next time I go to Jax Beach. And I won't have to worry about eating salads for a week.

CHAPTER 23

The Amelia Island Williams House

FERNANDINA BEACH

SEVERAL YEARS AGO our good friends, Liz and Warren Spahr, spent a weekend in the little Florida town of Fernandina Beach, which is tucked into the northeastern-most corner of the state. They stayed at the Amelia Island Williams House, one of the premier bed-and-breakfast inns in town.

They were sleeping in what is now the Egmont Indigo Suite when Liz was awakened by a little girl, perhaps ten or eleven, standing beside the bed. The child wore a frilly Victorian dress and a big bow in her long, curly hair, and she was smiling. She looked at Liz and asked, "What's your name?"

Liz wasn't at all frightened and replied, "Liz. What's yours?"

The girl answered, but Liz couldn't quite make out what she said—perhaps it was perhaps "Sally." She did recall that it had two syllables and ended with an "e" sound. Then the little girl laughed, danced around the room for about five seconds, and evaporated.

I remembered that story as I began to plan for this book, and now Sue and I found ourselves driving east along The Buccaneer Trail, Highway 200, to Fernandina Beach for an appointment with Byron and Deborah McCutchen, the owners of the Williams House.

I don't think I have ever seen an old inn so lovingly and carefully restored. From the original 1856 iron fence to the one-of-a kind 1860 gingerbread on the porch, every part of the house, inside and out, has been painstakingly repaired, replenished, and made like new.

We were welcomed on the front porch by Cinnamon, the cat. Then Byron invited us in and seated us comfortably in the parlor. He had a lot to tell us about paranormal activity in the Williams House, but first he gave us the history of this beautiful place.

The house was actually built in 1856 by a Boston banker but was purchased by Marcellus Williams, a successful surveyor, in 1859. A south wing was added in 1860. During the Civil War, Williams, a friend of Jefferson Davis, moved his family to Waldo, near Gainesville, to avoid contact with Union troops. The house in Fernandina was occupied by the Union forces and used as an infirmary, so it wasn't ransacked as were many of the homes in the area. After the war, Marcellus returned, and he and his heirs lived there for over one hundred years. And so the Williams name stuck to the house.

For almost fifty years after the last Williams resided there, the house was the private residence of Thomas and Gertrude Blatchford. In 1993 Chris Carter and Dick Flitz purchased the home, restored it to its original splendor, and opened it as a bed-and-breakfast. Byron and Deborah McCutchen have continued to maintain the sprawling house in pristine condition.

Byron, a chemical engineer before he and his wife bought the B&B, told us that he had always been skeptical about ghosts and the paranormal in general. From the beginning he kept a journal of the strange things that happened to him and to Deborah, as well as occurrences that guests reported.

One of the first things that happened to the McCutchens involved the candleholders on the parlor mantle. I looked at them as Byron was telling us the story. Both the mantle and the candleholders were sturdy, solid. Soon after taking over the B&B, Deborah came into the room in the morning several times to find the candles on the floor. She thought it odd but didn't say anything. One December evening, the McCutchens were sitting down with guests in the parlor for a glass of wine, and the candles rose out of the holders, flew through the air, and landed six feet away in front of the guests. "How did you do that?" The guests were astonished. So were Byron and Deborah.

A few days later, they began decorating for Christmas. Deborah was arranging poinsettia blossoms into garlands and hanging them in the foyer. She ran out of the red pipe stem cleaners she was using to fasten the blossoms. She climbed down from her ladder to get more, but they had disappeared from the foyer table where she'd put them. Exasperated, Deborah looked all over and couldn't locate them. Finally, she went out and bought more. A few days later, while cleaning in the dining room, she found her lost pipe cleaners—standing on end by a leg of the dining room table. Byron also was hanging garlands in the dining room during this same period and saw strange, dark shadows several times in the mirror as he was placing the garlands in position.

Deborah has had other experiences in the dining room. She has a beautiful voice, and her daughter, who was soon to marry, asked her to sing a solo at the wedding. Deborah was in the dining room practicing with sheet music and an instrumental tape of the piece. The phone rang and she went to answer it. When she returned, just as she was about to open the dining room door, she heard a girl's lovely voice singing with the tape. Deborah listened for a few minutes. When she finally opened the door, the singing stopped. Of course, no one was there. Deborah smiled, "Would you like to sing a duet?"

Not all the activity seems to be restricted to the inside of the home. The Williams House is a popular location for weddings. Once a photographer was taking digital pictures of couples sitting on the porch swing. After he finished, he and several others looked at the pictures. The first few were perfect. In the next, however, a blurry form, a silvery silhouette of a human, appeared moving in front of the couple on the swing.

Most of the activity, however, occurs inside and especially in the Egmont Indigo Suite. One of the housekeepers was looking after the inn while Byron and Deborah were away and stayed with her eight-month-old baby in the Egmont. The first evening, she had placed her son in a child's bouncy chair and was getting ready for bed. The baby started laughing, and when she looked, his head was turned and he was staring at one corner of the room. Odd, she thought, but she repositioned his little chair so that he was looking directly at her. Immediately, he faced back toward the corner and began laughing. Then the door to the room, which had been open, closed abruptly. She walked over to look out into the hall. No one was there. When she came back into the room, her son was still staring at the corner and laughing. Was he being entertained by the same happy little girl whom Liz had met?

The Williams had nine children and their progeny many more, not all of whom lived to adulthood. It seems that some of them are still there in the house. One guest was awakened early in the morning by the sound of a door slamming across the hall. When he got up to see what the commotion was, he heard what sounded like children laughing and playing downstairs. He saw nothing in the hall or any lights below. The next morning he learned from the innkeepers that he was the only guest, and there definitely had been no children in the inn.

Other guests also staying in the Egmont Indigo Suite on a later occasions reported the same thing. They heard a slamming door and children laughing below. They saw nothing when they went into the hall, and when they leaned over the stair rail, they saw no movement, although they continued to hear children's voices. In the morning, Byron and Deborah assured them that they were the only guests that night.

During the restoration by the original developers, a young girl appeared seated at the top of the staircase on the second floor, her legs dangling between the banisters. She just sat there smiling, looking at the men, and then disappeared. Was this also the little girl that Liz saw?

For many years, a little girl has been seen or heard by many guests, and for many years everyone thought that this child was probably Sally Williams. But not long ago Byron researched the Williams family and learned that Sally had actually lived until she was twenty. On the other hand, another daughter, Farey, had died at a young age in the house. Could Liz have mistaken "Sally" for "Farey?" Whoever the little girl is, she seems very happy to be in the Williams House.

Children are not the only entities there, however. One early morning, a well-dressed man in a gray suit, hat in hand, appeared at the end of Chris and Dick's bed, just standing there, then faded away. In the morning they began to look through old photographs to try to identify him. They soon found one that looked exactly like the man in the suit. It was the Williams' son, Marcellus Williams, Jr. He apparently liked Chris and Dick. They saw him several times during the years they owned the inn.

Perhaps it is Mr. Williams, the younger, who appears often in the King Ferdinand Royal Hideaway. One couple staying there was awakened by the sound of chains being dragged across the floor. When they sat up, the sound ceased. "You'll have to do better than that to scare us," they said and went back to sleep.

Another couple in the same room awoke when a man appeared and said, "I'm taking the strawberries now." The woman, not at all frightened, replied, "Fine, we're finished." And he took the strawberry dish. The next morning at breakfast, she asked Byron if he'd been in the room during the night. Of course he hadn't. And her husband also reminded her that the dead bolt on the door had been locked from the inside.

These are just a few of the incidents Byron has recorded in his "ghost" journal. He, Deborah, and their guests all seem to be quite comfortable with the happy spirits of the Williams House. And no wonder, it is a warm and loving environment. In fact, Sue and I are planning to go back for a weekend. Perhaps Mr. Williams or his little sister, Farey, will entertain us.

CHAPTER 24

Olustee Battlefield Historic State Park

Olustee

FRIDAY NIGHT. I was checking out potential ghost sites on the Internet when I came across the Olustee Battlefield Historic State Park in north Florida. It was the scene of the only major battle in Florida during the Civil War—and it was said to be haunted! The following day there was to be a Civil War Expo at the park. Excited, I picked up the phone and called Joanne. "What are you doing tomorrow?" I asked. With some hesitation, she replied, "I don't know. It sounds like you have something planned."

"You got it. Grab your camera and a notebook—we're going to meet some Civil War ghosts." Bright and early Saturday morning I picked up Joanne and her daughters, and we were headed off on another great road trip.

In February 1864, a Union army of over five thousand troops mounted an expedition out of occupied Jacksonville to cut off supplies, especially cattle, from Confederate forces to the North. The army's objective was Lake City, fifty miles away. As the Federals prepared to advance, Confederate General Joseph Finegan moved his army of five thousand to an area just east of Olustee, along the Lake City-Jacksonville Road, which ran roughly parallel to the Florida Atlantic and Gulf Central Railroad. There, between a cypress swamp and Ocean Pond, his troops began establishing defensive positions.

By mid-afternoon of the February 20, the Union forces closed with Finegan's army, and the battle was joined. The fighting was vicious and deadly. The terrain was flat and relatively open, except for the widely-spaced pine trees. Frequently, combat was hand-to-hand. The ground between Ocean Pond and the cypress swamp was red with the blood of the dead and dying. The struggle surged back and forth, but by late afternoon, the Confederates mounted a charge that the Union army couldn't stop. General Seymour, the Federal general, finally admitted defeat and started his retreat back to Jacksonville.

Almost two thousand Union troops died, were wounded, or were missing, and the Confederates lost nearly one thousand. Percentage-wise, Olustee was the third bloodiest battle for the Union Army during the Civil War.

In 1912, the governor of Florida designated the Olustee Battlefield Florida's first state park. In those early years, many Civil War veterans and survivors of the Olustee battle attended reunions there. Today, to commemorate the battle, a reenactment is held every February as close to the 20th as possible, and the Civil War Expo takes place in late summer.

We arrived at the park by mid-morning. Crowds were already starting to gather. Unlike the reenactment in February when hundreds of reenactors participate, the Expo has no more than fifty or sixty. Still, the atmosphere was historic with Confederate and Union infantry, cavalry, civilian refugees, and sutler's camps. There were infantry and cavalry drills, musket and artillery firing demonstrations, small skirmishes, and period music. But the best was the Battlefield Trail, which ran in front of what had been the Confederate lines, around the swamp, back down in front of the Union lines, and around Ocean Pond.

Joanne and I left the busyness and noise of the Expo behind as we began walking down the trail. A strange quiet descended. The day was warm, but we were cooled by the shade of the many pine trees on the battlefield—or was the change in temperature something else? In many places, the area is now thick with palmetto and other ground cover, and as we walked, a sense of dread began to overtake us. Joanne, especially, started to react. I could see the goose bumps forming on her arms. Her breathing became labored.

"Are you okay?" I asked as I became concerned. She half-smiled. "No, I'm not. There is so much negative energy here. It's almost overpowering. I feel like I have a ton of bricks on my shoulders."

We walked a little further, and I could see she was getting worse. "Look. Why don't you go on back. Go talk to some of the reenactors. They'll have some stories," I said.

She stood there, silent for some time. "I guess you're right. I'll go back." She turned to go, but hesitated and turned around. With a sheepish smile she asked, "Will you walk back down the trail with me. I don't want to go by myself."

I walked her back to the Expo and turned once again to go up the trail. I would like to say that I had some eventful experi-

Late-night walks around the battlefield are popular with Civil War reenactors, who have seen a ghost or two in this historic park.

ences, but I didn't. The walk around the battlefield was pleasant, if a little eerie, but that was it for me.

When I returned to the Expo, I spied Joanne across the field talking to several reenactors from the Tenth Tennessee Cavalry. I decided to interview some others. I soon came to the encampment of Camp 1463 of the Sons of Confederate Veterans from Olustee.

Private Dave Murphree and Captain Dave Eversol, both long-time participants in the February reenactment, were willing to talk. Even though the Expo was only a one-day affair, the reenactors had all camped overnight. The previous night they had sat around their campfire, telling stories, and listening to one of their group play his "cigar box" fiddle until late in the evening. About two in the morning, they decided to go for a walk around the area to see what they could "scare up." Apparently, late-night walks around battlefields are popular with reenactors.

The moon was not very bright, so they carried a Civil War-era lantern as they left their encampment and headed for the brush and trees on the far side of the open area. They were, of course, wearing Confederate uniforms. As they approached, they both saw someone step out of the underbrush, stare at them for a moment, and then melt back into the scrub. In the dim light they couldn't tell much about the person, except that they thought it was a man, and he was wearing dark clothes and a slouch hat. They thought it was probably some vagrant camping out in the woods.

Continuing along, they were startled to see what they thought was the same man appear suddenly out of the scrub, look at them, and fade back into the bushes. A little unsettled now, they continued their walk another hundred yards or so and again saw the man in the dark clothes and slouch hat. At that point, they both remembered that the park was five miles away from any-where—it wasn't a hangout for the homeless. And that slouch hat. They both felt they'd seen a ghost. Rattled, they turned and headed quick time back to camp.

During the 2005 February reenactment, on a bitterly cold morning, Captain Eversol crawled out of his tent to go to the latrine. The moon was bright, and a heavy mist covered the ground. As he walked along, hunkered down in his coat, another Confederate soldier wearing a slouch hat and open sack coat came out of a row of tents towards him. Captain Eversol thought at first that he was just another reenactor. He could see the man's CSA belt buckle. He looked down then and, somewhat surprised, saw that the man was barefoot. As he moved his gaze up to the man's face, the soldier evaporated into thin air. Eversol wasn't frightened at all by this. In fact, he had a comforting feeling of seeing just another brother in arms.

Andy Lee, a member of the Tenth Tennessee Cavalry and also a frequent participant in the February reenactment, had several good stories to tell. The first was about "Red Eyes," a Confederate soldier who died during the 1864 battle and was buried by his comrades on the battlefield with a rough wooden marker, which read simply "Red Eyes." Shortly after the burial, while Confederate troops still milled around, the marker disappeared, and his friends could not find it again.

Two years ago, a woman dressed as a cavalryman attended the reenactment with her husband. (During the Civil War there were many instances of women dressing as men and fighting alongside their husbands.) After they had set up camp, she went for a ride by herself through the surrounding woods and came across an old slab of wood. She dismounted and was just able to read the inscription carved on it, "Red Eyes." Excited, she removed her saddle blanket, put it over the marker to make it more visible, and galloped back to camp. She came back shortly with several of her comrades, but they were never able to relocate the saddle blanket or marker.

She returned the following summer for the Expo and was again riding in the woods, when she came to the spot where her blanket had disappeared. There lay the blanket—but no wooden slab.

Last year at the reenactment, a friend of Andy's, Jonathan Welsher, went for a daytime ride on the Battlefield Trail. As he rode along, a man's leg dressed in Union-blue trousers and a black boot shot out of the scrub and tripped Jonathan's horse, causing it to stumble and toss its rider to the ground. Before Jonathan could recover, a rifle butt smacked him in the jaw. There was not another human about. Dazed, he caught up his horse and rode back to camp. Andy and his friends rode back to the site. There were no human footprints and no sign of an attack, but Jonathan swore he was telling the truth, and Andy swore that the mark on Jonathan's face was the exact shape of the butt of a rifle.

Of course, not all encounters have been violent. During the Expo three years ago, a Confederate artillery unit was demonstrating firing when they ran low on gun powder. The crew chief sent Jim Tucker back to their campsite for more. As Jim trotted along, another Confederate soldier appeared from nowhere, handed Jim a box, and said, "Here. Take this. You'll need it." Jim sat the box down to open it and discovered bags of gunpowder. When he looked up to thank the man, he had disappeared.

Olustee is a great place for paranormal encounters, perhaps because of all the violent deaths that occurred there. Maybe some paranormal investigator can summon the courage to spend the night on this bloody battlefield. It would be exciting, to say the least.

The Panhandle

Apalachicola
Coombs House Inn

Monticello
Palmer House

Pensacola
Pensacola Lighthouse
Pensacola Victorian Bed-and-Breakfast
Seville Quarter

Quincy
Leaf Theatre

Tallahassee
Knott House Museum

CHAPTER 25

Palmer House
MONTICELLO

BY THE TIME I TURNED MY ATTENTION to the Florida Panhandle, I was starting to run out of contacts. Fortunately, I found the Big Bend Ghost Trackers, and Betty Davis and Lisa Guancial were only too happy to give me a hand.

Our first stop was Monticello, just east of Tallahassee, and the South's most haunted small town. One out of three homes and office buildings are said to be haunted, so we could have gone anywhere, but Betty and Lisa thought I would enjoy the Palmer House, formerly a doctor's residence and now an antique shop. I was happy that my antique-loving wife stayed home for this trip. Joanne Overly, the owner's daughter, was there to meet us and give us a tour.

Dr. Martin Palmer built the house in 1840. A loyal Confederate, he went off to the Civil War with his compatriots in 1861. Perhaps because of the carnage he witnessed as a surgeon or because the South had lost the war, Dr. Palmer returned to Monticello a despondent and broken old man. Not long after his return, he committed suicide in the house.

His son, Dabney, took over his practice, the fifth generation of Palmers to be a physician. The town folk considered Dr. Dabney Palmer unorthodox, by any standards. As was common in the day, Dr. Dabney was not just the town physician, but the mortician as well. His doctor's office was in a separate building in the front yard, but he maintained his mortuary facility on the second floor of the house. A former slave, Poltergeist, so called because everyone said he didn't cast a shadow, worked for Dr. Dabney. He carted remains to the cemetery in his mule-driven wagon, dug graves, and, some said, dug them up again for Dr. Dabney. The doctor had a bizarre belief that bodies should be buried with their blood, so he would drain blood from a body into a bucket, which Poltergeist would take to the cemetery and pour into the grave before interment. Presumably, he did so before anyone showed up for the funeral.

One day the doctor and Poltergeist got into an argument, probably about wages. Poltergeist became angry and threw a bucket of blood on Dr. Dabney. The blood not only covered the doctor but also splattered the wall. Through the ensuing years, no one was ever able to remove the blood stains from the wall. Numerous owners and renters tried stain killer, primer, paint, and wallpaper without success.

Jackie Andress, Joanne's mother, had a lifelong desire to own an antique store. Several years ago, her indulgent husband bought her the Palmer House to fulfill her dream. As she cleaned and renovated, she tried removing the blood stains from the wall in the room on the second floor. Like everyone else before her, she was unsuccessful. Then, she had an idea: She'd take out the whole wall and paint the room pink, which she did.

Finally, she opened her shop for business and immediately had customers. She had hung a portrait over the fireplace in what had been the Palmers' parlor, which was immediately below the Pink Room where the stained wall had been. One day a lady came in and wanted to buy the portrait. Jackie took it off the wall—and there were the blood stains. Somehow they had moved. Jackie has photos of the original stains, which exactly match the stains now in the old parlor.

Joanne took us upstairs to the Pink Room and told us of her experience there. After the wall had been removed, she was in the room and touched the now free-standing brick fireplace heating column. Instantly, she lost all color and felt as if the blood stains that had been on the now missing wall had shot through her. At the same time, she saw a bluish-purple, bearded man in a bedraggled, dark uniform with two rows of buttons down the front.

One Saturday after that experience, Joanne brought her little nephew, Coby, to the store with her. He had a great time running around the rooms, up and down the stairs, but when he went into the parlor, he stopped in front of the stain above the fireplace and asked, "Who is that monster?" "What monster, honey?" his aunt replied. Pointing, he said, "The one right there, the black and blue one." Joanne quickly ushered him out of the room.

One hot summer evening when Mrs. Andress was in the hall by the front door, Joanne, who was in the dining room, heard her mother talking to someone. She yelled down the hall, "Who are you talking to, Mom?" She walked into the hall to have a look for herself. Her mother stood alone in what looked like a shimmering heat wave. But when Joanne joined her mother, the area was icy cold.

Her mother simply replied, "'Miss Dorothy' wants the house." No one ever determined who "Miss Dorothy" was.

Joanne reported that strange things happen constantly. Her mother and countless patrons have heard people talking and walking around upstairs when no one else was there. Once, a teddy bear on a bed literally flew off the bed and onto the floor right in front of several people. A rocking chair in the back room rocks back and forth by itself, and a chandelier swings around for no reason.

Betty, Lisa, and the Big Bend Ghost Trackers have investigated the house on several occasions. On one of their first investigations, they had set up video equipment, thermal scanners, and audio recorders throughout the house. The chimes in the courthouse tower nearby were ringing three o'clock in the morning when they heard footsteps coming down the stairs. When they looked up the stairs, a large black mass was descending toward them. They couldn't figure out what it was, but it terrified them, and they fled outside. Betty, Lisa, and the others seriously considered leaving the five-hundred-thousand-dollars worth of equipment in the house and coming back the next day for it, but finally screwed up their courage, went back in, and finished their investigation, hearing something pacing back and forth upstairs the rest of the night. The next day when they viewed what the cameras had captured, they still couldn't identify the black mass coming down the stairs.

On another investigation, a film crew from the Florida State University Film School accompanied the BBGT investigators. Most of the students were skeptical when they arrived. They weren't when they left.

In what is known as the Purple Room in the Palmer House is a doll in an antique baby buggy. Neither Jackie nor Joanne remembers exactly where this particular doll came from, but everyone who sees it thinks it is spooky. Its eyes seem to follow you as you walk around the room.

This doll is an "effigy doll." In the late 1800s, it became the fashion to create some remembrance of people, especially children, when they died. Often it was a photograph of the dead child, but when photographers weren't available, parents would sometimes take hair, eyebrows, and even plaster of Paris castings of the child's face and give the items to a doll maker to create an exact likeness.

Like many paranormal investigating groups, BBGT has certain protocols they require of their investigators. One of Betty's first rules is that no one investigates alone. She requires at least two people to enter an area, both as a matter of safety and as a means of verification.

On this occasion, BBGT member Valynda Nicholas was so excited by the effigy doll that she went into the Purple Room by herself. At that point, Betty was listening to her radio and heard a scream. She and several others rushed upstairs to find Valynda pale and shaking outside the room. Something had grabbed her neck as she had entered. Betty said she could still see the fingerprints. After Valynda had calmed down, she said she didn't feel that anything was trying to harm her. It was just trying to warn her to stay out of the room. She and the others learned a valuable lesson about following protocol, and the FSU film crew became believers.

Betty and her ghost trackers have had many experiences in the Palmer House, and Joanne and her mother daily encounter things they can't explain. Even though they've been frightened from time to time, nothing in the house seems to be really harmful. And in a way, it's comforting to know that they're not alone, even when they're there all by themselves.

CHAPTER 26

Knott House Museum

TALLAHASSEE

AFTER A DELICIOUS LUNCH of pizza at the Monticello Pizza Kitchen, which, by the way, is also haunted, Betty, Lisa, and I headed for Tallahassee and the Knott House Museum just down from Florida's Old Capitol in the Park Avenue Historic District.

The area around what is now Tallahassee has been occupied by various indigenous and European cultures for twelve thousand years. Soon after the United States took possession of Florida from the Spanish in 1821, the Territorial Governor, William P. Duval, laid out the city, and in 1824 it became the territorial and later state capital of Florida. It is a beautiful city. Its rolling hills, wide boulevards, stately buildings, various college campuses, and numerous parks give Tallahassee a genteel ambiance. And the Knott House with its handsome Greek Revival facade only adds to that atmosphere.

The house was built in 1843 by free-black builder George Proctor as a wedding gift for Thomas Hagner and his wife, Catherine. Thomas died in 1848, but Catherine remained in the house and added major additions to the rear. She turned it into a boarding house, presumably to supplement her income. At the end of the Civil War, Union General Edward McCook commandeered the home for his headquarters. He read President Lincoln's Emancipation Proclamation from the front steps on May 20, 1865. Today a ceremony on May 20 every year commemorates the event.

The Hagner family owned the house until 1883 when they sold it to a Dr. Betton, who maintained his office in the building. Following a succession of owners, William and Luella Knott finally bought the house in 1928. The Knotts were an influential family in Tallahassee. William was variously the state treasurer and comptroller and ran unsuccessfully for governor. Luella, a poet and community volunteer, was a staunch supporter of women's rights. She homeschooled her three children, Mary Franklin, James Robert, and John Charles ("Charlie"), wrote and published countless poems, and filled her house with the antiques she loved. She also filled her home with poetry, which even today is scattered around the rooms, tied to various items with silk ribbons. Because of that, the house is known as the "The House That Rhymes."

William died in April 1965 at 101 years of age; Luella fell and died a few days after that. Charlie then moved into his family home, determined to preserve it as his parents had left it. And when he died in 1985, he left it to the State of Florida, stipulating that it be maintained as a museum house. The Historic Tallahassee Preservation Board took charge of the property, and after spending more than one million dollars and several years of preservation and restoration efforts—the restoration team found evidence of earlier fires, which had to be addressed—the museum finally opened to the public in 1992.

Walking through the house is eerie. It is so complete and looks so lived in, I expected to see the lady of the house, Mrs. Knott, around every corner and in every room. There are four thousand books, three hundred pieces of furniture, and fifteen hundred personal items and art work. Books lie open on tables. Personal effects are strewn about. I would not have been surprised to see a steaming cup of coffee sitting on the counter in the kitchen, waiting for Charlie to come in and pick it up. I felt as if I were invading the Knotts' privacy, as if I shouldn't be there. But it is a beautiful house and extremely well maintained. Tours in the past used to be self-guided, but are now led by knowledgeable docents. That's probably a good idea.

Betty and her BBGT crew have been through the house many times. In past years, the curator hosted a "Fear Knott" event around Halloween as a fund-raiser. Betty, Lisa, and their team gave presentations and "haunted" tours through the house in the evenings. They also have conducted paranormal investigations in the building and have spent many nights there after the museum was closed.

The most frequent experiences reported by BBGT investigators, visitors, and staff are footsteps. They are heard throughout the house. Sometimes they are very heavy like a man's, and at other times lighter, as if a woman were walking around. They could very well be Charlie's father, his mother, or Charlie himself. All three had a special passion for the house.

Once in the days when the tours were self-guided, a visitor rushed down the stairs breathless. A staff member was standing at the bottom. The visitor, quite excited, said, "I believe I've just seen a ghost!"

The staff member, who'd had her own experiences, asked the lady what had happened. "Well, I just went into the first room on the right at the top of the stairs, and there was an older woman dressed in old-fashioned clothes standing there. At first, I thought she was a docent or something, but she just stood there and looked at me. And then she evaporated into thin air!"

On several other occasions, visitors have reported seeing people throughout the house who appeared to be visitors as well, only to vanish before their eyes. Perhaps Charlie, his parents, and maybe even his friends are walking the halls.

In the past, various staff members have reported items being moved around. Perhaps a book has been taken from a shelf in the library and left on a table somewhere else, pictures rearranged, fireplace tools misplaced, pages of music on the piano turned. At the end of each day, the outside doors to the Knott House are closed and locked, of course, but inside doors are always left open to provide air circulation. Often when staff members arrive in the morning to unlock the house, those inside doors are all closed. And passersby late at night have reported seeing lights switching on and off inside the locked and empty house, as if someone was going from room to room.

In the Knott House, Betty and her BBGT investigators have experienced just about every activity others have reported. They've also had another experience. During one investigation, Betty and Lisa were sitting downstairs, quietly listening, when they heard humming coming from upstairs. It sounded like a woman softly humming a lullaby to a baby. When they went through every room in the house to try to find the source of the sound, they could hear it everywhere but were never able to identify its location.

The Knott House Museum is a "must-see" stop for anyone visiting Tallahassee. The visitor will find the most completely restored nineteenth-century house in Florida, and who knows? You might get to meet Mr. and Mrs. Knott or their son, Charlie.

CHAPTER 27

Leaf Theatre
QUINCY

RURAL FLORIDA in the mid-twentieth century was a pretty quiet place. The primary industry around most towns was agriculture, and people worked so hard they didn't have much time for frivolities and entertainment. But one thing most towns, even very small ones, had was a movie theater. Quincy, in the Panhandle's Gadsden County, was no different. It had the Leaf Theatre, so named because the major crop in the county was shade tobacco.

The Leaf was built in 1949, between World War II and the Korean War, when things had settled down. There wasn't much else to do in Quincy on Saturday night except go to the local juke joint or the "movin' theater." The Leaf was large, with 990 seats, including the balcony, a spacious entrance and lobby, restrooms, and a concession stand. It was the social center of town where people met to get the local gossip and catch up, and, of course, the weekly newsreels kept everyone up to date on national and world news.

The Leaf Theatre did well for over twenty-five years, but attendance gradually fell off as alternatives evolved. By the 1970s, most people had cars and could easily travel into Tallahassee and other nearby towns, and TV by then was a major source of entertainment. So the Leaf closed in 1978 and sat vacant except for an occasional gospel show or revival meeting. But most of the time, the building remained empty and deteriorating, its roof beginning to leak badly and the interior shabby and decaying.

In February 1983, local citizens formed the Quincy Music Theatre, QMT, holding their kickoff production in the First Presbyterian Church in July. In December, with private funding, the QMT purchased the dilapidated old Leaf and performed *Lil' Abner* there, leaking roof, tiny stage, and all.

Through the years, the QMT has renovated the Leaf into a first class theater, one of the best community theaters in the state. Volunteers removed several rows of front seats and expanded the stage, closed off the projection booth, revamped the balcony and installed new seats, added dressing rooms, storage space, workshops for building sets, and upgraded the lighting. One thing the crew did not change was the front entrance. The ticket office, lobby, and concession stand remain as they were in 1949, and the theater still feels and looks much like the old Leaf.

After Betty, Lisa, and I left the Knott House in Tallahassee, we came straight over to Quincy to meet with Bill Mock, the current QMT director. Bill had been a volunteer for many years before he became the director and was intimately familiar with the Leaf and its history.

Betty and Lisa had been there many times before and had conducted several investigations, so they and Bill were old friends. After introductions, the three took me on a tour of the inner workings and hidden mechanisms—and mysteries—of this live-performance theater.

Bill had long suspected that the Leaf was haunted. An actress, who was also psychic and who performed with the QMT at the Leaf, saw a man in the theater during rehearsals. She mentioned it, but no one else could see him. He had light brown hair, khaki trousers, a brown belt, and a brown felt hat, and he kept staring anxiously at his watch. She also saw a young boy who was obviously an apparition.

A previous director once was frightened by a female apparition, perhaps the mother of a former owner. Others have seen the young boy and also a little girl. A cleaning lady had eventually been so frightened that she quit and never set foot in the theater again. She had often heard music when there was no one else in the building, and on several occasions she had seen an angry-looking man in the balcony. She had called out to him to ask what he was doing there, and he had disappeared before her eyes. She also claimed to have seen people in the theater, including the slightly balding, brown-haired man in khaki trousers sitting in the third seat of the front row. Curiously, that seat to this day will not stay up, even though there seems to be nothing wrong with the spring mechanism.

Over time, the cleaning lady became understandably uncomfortable, but one day while she was upstairs in the balcony, a man approached from the far right corner—and walked right through her. Terrified, she screamed, dropped her broom, and rushed downstairs and out of the building. She never returned, not even to pick up her pay.

Members of the QMT still see and hear things all the time. Once, Bill was working late in an area offstage. He thought he

**A cleaning lady saw an angry-looking man in the balcony—presumably
a ghost.**

was alone, but he heard someone begin to play the piano and
figured that Kevin, another member, had come in and started
playing. After a few minutes, the music stopped. He didn't hear
any footsteps, so he went up to see what Kevin was up to. Kevin
wasn't there, and the piano was covered. Bill found out later that
Kevin hadn't been in the theater that evening.

On another occasion Bill had lain down on a couch in his
office for a quick nap. He was awakened by someone lying down
very close to him. When he opened his eyes, he was alone on the
couch and saw no one in the room.

David Jones was working on a tall ladder on stage when
he heard children behind him in the theater. When he turned
around to see who was there, a boy and a girl both about ten or
twelve and wearing what he thought were 1940s or '50s clothes
were sitting in the middle of the theater, giggling and talking to

each other. When they saw him looking at them, they vanished.

Several members have seen a female apparition in the lobby or in the rear of the theater during shows, as well as a little girl in the hallway and lobby. There are cold spots all over the theater, especially on the stairs leading up to the balcony. Tools disappear and are found in strange locations.

On one of BBGTs investigations, Betty was sitting quietly meditating, waiting for something to happen. The name "Gibson" came to mind, and as she was thinking about what that meant, she saw a short, stocky, slightly balding man with light brown hair, wearing khaki trousers and holding a hat. He, too, seemed to be obsessed with his watch, looking at it over and over again. Another BBGT team member, Lacey, was sitting with Betty and also picked up the name "Charlie." That same evening Lisa and others in the group captured several orbs in photos around the theater, but especially on the stage.

The report of this investigation made the local newspaper. A few weeks later, William Dickson called Betty about the article. He had grown up with Charles ("Charlie") MacDonald, the son of the projectionist at the Leaf for many years, Sherille Odel "Mac" MacDonald. He and Charles were still close friends. He indicated that they'd like to come and look over the old theater, because as boys they both had spent a lot of time there. A meeting was arranged.

Bill, Betty, and Lisa met Charles, William, and their wives in the lobby and gave them a tour of the building. Charles was especially touched seeing the place where his father had spent so much of his life. And when he showed them an old photo of his father, Betty was astounded at how precise her vision of the man in the khaki trousers was, even down to the watch.

She asked Charles about the watch, why his father seemed so obsessed with it. He explained that his dad, Mac, not only ran the projectors but also made sure that the crowd cleared the theater in time for the next showing. He explained, too, that in those early days, films came in cylindrical cans; one movie might be in four or five or more cans, and they were passed around from theater to theater. When one theater finished showing a film, it rushed the cans to the next. If they were late, the movie would be late starting at the next theater, with a domino effect down the line. So the projectionists, especially his father, were sometimes paranoid about staying on schedule.

He also talked about his relationship with his father. The Leaf was Mac's life, so much so that it destroyed his marriage. He and his wife divorced, and Charles and his mother moved away. He hadn't seen much of his father and wasn't with him when he died in 1981. He had the distinct impression that per-haps all of this—BBGT's investigation, the newspaper article, and his visit—had all been instigated by his father to tell him that everything was fine between them.

And, what about the name Gibson? Betty was still puzzled by that. "Oh, The Gibson was a theater in Chattahoochee where Dad worked as a young man," said Charles.

As a final validation, another cleaning lady, Bobbie, saw an angry black man in the balcony on the right and also the man in khaki trousers and brown hat on the stage. Sometime later she was in Bill's office and happened to see a photograph of "Mac" MacDonald, which Charles had left with Bill. "That's the man," she said, pointing at the picture. "That's the man I saw on the stage."

The Leaf Theatre is definitely a haunted place, and it has the papers to prove it.

CHAPTER 28

Coombs House Inn

APALACHICOLA

APALACHICOLA IS ONE OF THOSE you-can't-get-there-from-here kind of places, and I was glad to have my Big Bend Ghost Trackers friends, Betty and Lisa, with me on the long drive down from Quincy through the Apalachicola National Forest.

The town has had a long and colorful history. Settled in 1821 when the United States gained possession of Florida from Spain, it became the third-largest port on the Gulf by 1837, shipping cotton to destinations around the world. The Union blockade destroyed the cotton trade during the Civil War, but Apalachicola survived.

James Coombs had spent most of his young life in the timber industry in Maine, where he was born in 1842. When the

Civil War started, he joined the Union forces and spent time in the Deep South. After the war, he returned to Maine, married his childhood sweetheart, Marie Starrett, and went on with his career in timber. But he remembered the vast forests in the South and saw opportunity. The War Between the States had ravaged much of the infrastructure throughout the South, and vast amounts of lumber were needed to rebuild. In 1871 he brought his family first to Pensacola and then in 1877 to Apalachicola, where in the ensuing years he made a fortune.

By the turn of the century, Coombs was a wealthy and influential man. In 1900, he declined the nomination for Governor of Florida and in 1904 he turned down Teddy Roosevelt's offer to be his running mate.

Sixty-two years old and at the pinnacle of his career, he decided that he and his family needed a new home to reflect his status. And the house he built was grand, with nine fireplaces, including one in the entryway hall, a wraparound porch and second-floor balcony, a widow's walk, a forty-two-inch front door to accommodate a coffin for wakes, carved oak banisters, black cypress wall paneling, indoor plumbing, leaded-glass windows, brass light fixtures, and glistening oak floors. It was one of the most spectacular homes in Apalachicola.

But tragedy struck the Coombs family in 1911, just five years after they had moved into the house. A fire started at about midnight on March 6. While the damage from the fire was significant, the efforts of the volunteer fire companies fighting the blaze all but demolished the house. Furniture, drapes, bedding, clothes were thrown into soggy piles in the yard. Exquisite wooden floors and paneling were drenched and swollen. Everything was ruined.

Mr. and Mrs. Coombs spent the night in the nearby Franklin Hotel, intending to rebuild their home, but Mrs. Coombs became ill and was taken to the hospital. She died, some say of a broken heart, ten days later. Mr. Coombs died three weeks after that. They both were buried in the Chestnut Street Cemetery across from their cherished home.

During most of the next eighty years, the house stood boarded up, empty, and forlorn, except for the occasional vagrant who broke into the place. The rear balcony collapsed. Windows were broken. Siding, floors, and wood paneling rotted away. The town considered demolishing the building.

But in 1978, Bill Spohrer and has wife, Lynn Wilson, came to Apalachicola and saw the old Coombs house. Lynn, a well-known interior designer who had renovated the Biltmore in Coral Gables and the Vinoy Hotel in St. Petersburg, immediately saw the potential in the Coombs home and set about buying it. Because Coombs family members were so scattered, it took her twelve years to acquire it.

In the following months, Lynn hired local craftsman and began renovating the house. Restoring as much of the house as she could to the original condition, she also designed some tasteful additions, including eleven new bathrooms and a modern kitchen. She replaced windows, rebuilt balconies, and installed new beams. She redid the floors and replaced the beautiful, old wall paneling. When she was finished with the work, she furnished the house with exquisite antiques and paintings from the early 1900s, many from her own collection. And, with one final masterful stroke—she painted the house yellow! At first, some townspeople were shocked, but everyone had to admit that it was dazzling. The bright yellow inn has since become a landmark in Apalachicola.

The Coombs Inn opened in August of 1994, but even before any guests entered, Bill and Lynn realized there was something unusual about the house. Of course, they knew all about the fire and Mr. and Mrs. Coombs, but they hadn't considered any paranormal activity. However, during the renovation, workmen would sometimes notice that closed doors were later found open and open doors closed. Tools and materials would be moved. Occasionally, a carpenter working on the first floor heard children laughing upstairs. All these incidents were so subtle and innocuous, no one thought that much about them or that the house might be haunted.

Over the years, however, people began to have more obvious experiences. Anna Wilson, a former innkeeper, reportedly saw Mr. Coombs during Hurricane Dennis. Estelle Banta, a former manager, remembered that Anna had called to her from the dining room and said that she'd just seen Mr. Coombs. He was on the porch and was trying to get in. Later during the storm, Anna saw him again in the same place, and he walked right through a wall. She knew it was Mr. Coombs. She recognized him from his picture hanging in the dining room.

Estelle said that she personally had never seen a ghost, but she had heard children playing upstairs, and one of the housekeepers reported that she'd seen them. Estelle had also found guests' notes in the journals kept in each room relating stories of apparitions (one guest reportedly saw Mrs. Coombs), strange noises, and feelings of someone standing at the foot of the bed. There were several entries in journals, reporting that someone had brushed or kissed their cheeks during the night. And a local young man, Tommy Sanchez, told the Spohrers that in the '70s he had gone into the house and seen Mrs. Coombs.

No one was ever particularly bothered by any of their experiences, but after several years of so many reports, Lynn wanted to know if anything paranormal was truly going on, so she called Betty Davis. And that's how the Big Bend Ghost Trackers first came to the Coombs Inn to do an investigation. They have since been several times.

Lisa Guancial was one of the first investigators in the house. She, like many others, heard children laughing and playing in the attic, and during the night she stayed in the inn, she saw a little boy in the hallway. Curiously, Lynn said that several years before while she was wandering through the house, she had discovered a hidden passage behind a chair in the entryway. When she was able to pry the door open, she went in and discovered old children's toys. The passage obviously had not been entered in decades.

Lisa also reported that twice during her night in Mr. and Mrs. Coombs' old bedroom, someone had entered and then left. The first time, the door opened by itself and closed. She could feel someone in the room but couldn't see anything. The second time, someone came into the room, the door opening and closing by itself, and stood at the end of the bed. Lisa couldn't tell if it was a man or a woman, but she knew positively that it wasn't a live, breathing human being. She also felt the back of a hand softly brush her cheek.

BBGT investigators have also heard inexplicable footsteps, seen lights turn on and off, and heard voices. They have even tied doors shut only to find them untied and open the following morning.

When Betty, Lisa, and I arrived after our drive from Quincy, it was happy hour, and the house was full. A group of young folks from the Tampa Bay area were staying for a weekend excursion. When they discovered we were there about ghosts, they were all ears. Lynn led us around, showing all the rooms and telling stories about the house. Her guests were only too happy to open their rooms for us. At one point, Lynn and I sat talking in Mr. and Mrs. Coombs' room, and I got a distinct impression of someone else's presence. It was a comforting feeling.

When we finally departed and headed back to Tallahassee, I was reluctant to leave. I vowed then that as soon as this haunted road trip was over, I was bringing Sue back here for our own weekend excursion. I'd like to enjoy more of Lynn and Bill's warm hospitality—and I'd really like to meet Mr. and Mrs. Coombs.

CHAPTER 29

Pensacola Victorian Bed-and-Breakfast

PENSACOLA

I WAS NEARING THE END of my haunted road trip across Florida, and Sue and I began planning one last foray to the far end of the Panhandle—to Pensacola. Since it was to be our last trip, and I knew we'd have to spend several days there, I wanted it to be an especially enjoyable one for Sue, to reward her for all the effort she'd put into this book.

We always stay in bed-and-breakfasts, if we can, so Sue got on the Internet and began looking for accommodations. She picked the Pensacola Victorian Bed-and-Breakfast in downtown Pensacola. When she made the reservations, she told the owner, Barbee Major, what we were up to. Barbee said that she and her husband, Chuck, had ghosts in the B&B. That got my attention. I had planned on several other sites based on my preliminary research, but I at least wanted to talk to Barbee about her hauntings.

The grand, old Victorian house at 203 West Gregory Street was built in 1872 by Captain William Northup, a wealthy ship's captain from Kingston, Rhode Island. He and his brother-in-law, E. E. Saunders, had come to Pensacola to expand their businesses. Among other things, Captain Northup shipped timber around the world, and when he could, he used Italian granite for ballast on return trips. That's why his house is the only one in Pensacola which has a granite foundation.

Northup became a leading citizen of Pensacola, serving as postmaster, customs collector, councilman, and mayor. His house served as a gathering place for Pensacola's elite. Northup died in 1925, but his son, Edwin, and Edwin's wife, Louise, moved into the house and carried on the Captain's tradition.

Edwin was an excellent musician, proficient on several instruments, including the violin and the coronet. Louise played piano. An engineer, Edwin worked in the Brooklyn Naval Shipyard for a time and often had informal gatherings after work to play classical music. When he and Louise took over the house in Pensacola, they continued the get-togethers. They even brought in two grand pianos, which nearly filled the music room. These sessions eventually led to the creation of the Pensacola Philharmonic Orchestra in 1926.

The Majors' acquisition of the house can only be considered amazing. They had visited Pensacola almost annually for over twenty years, so they knew the town well. In 1995, they were restaurateurs in St. Louis when Barbee was diagnosed with cancer. They sold their restaurant and began to think of relocating to Pensacola, where Barbee's sister already lived. With her sister's encouragement, they made their decision to move.

They weren't sure what they'd do to support themselves, but Barbee had lived most of her life near water and was thinking about opening a waterfront restaurant. The week before they left St. Louis, Barbee's best friend had a dream. She saw Barbee in a huge Victorian house. People were drinking tea. And her friend described the house in detail—outside and in.

Shortly after arriving in Pensacola, Chuck happened to see a listing in a local real estate magazine. The place wasn't listed as a bed-and-breakfast, and the price was out of their range, but they decided to have a look anyway. The owners met them at the door, and as soon as Barbee entered, she knew she was home. The house was exactly as her friend had described.

The owners accepted their offer, which was much less than the asking price, but the Majors were still short a considerable amount for a down payment. At the last minute, however, just before closing, friends came forth and provided what they needed. Soon after, they opened the B&B.

From the beginning, inexplicable things happened. Barbee often heard what sounded like a woman working in the kitchen, dishes rattling, cabinet drawers opening and closing, pots being placed on a stove, children laughing and playing, the gentle, unintelligible prattle of a mother talking to her little ones. Barbee and her guests also have heard the sounds of dishes smashing on the floor and the sounds of an argument or at least a not-so-amicable discussion. No one has ever determined the specific location of those noises.

At breakfast one morning, a playwright staying in the inn asked rather sheepishly if any ghosts inhabited the place. Barbee admitted that they probably did. As Barbee and her other guests nodded, the young man related that during the night he had gotten up to go to the bathroom and was astounded to see a woman in a long, white wrapper walk soundlessly into the bathroom ahead of him. Confused for a moment, he hesitated to follow her. Then he thought, well, she didn't close the door, so I must be hallucinating. He shrugged and went in. No one was there.

Barbee suggested that we contact her friend, Sharon Renae, a local spiritualist, medium, writer, and ordained minister. Sharon has been to the B&B many times and has had the same experiences as Barbee and many of her guests. She's also had some of her own.

On one occasion, she was upstairs in the turret bedroom putting on makeup for a television pilot she was filming. She sensed someone looking at her. Reflected behind her in the mirror was a small hand wrapped around the edge of the open door. She couldn't see the whole apparition because it was peeking around the door jamb, but she knew from the size of the hand that it had to be a child or perhaps a young woman, watching inquisitively while she continued getting ready. Later, she saw what she believed was the same small entity on the staircase coming up from the front parlor.

Sharon conducts spiritual counseling and at one session a client told her about a dream she'd had. In the dream she saw the parlor of a large Victorian house. Several people sat around, and a number of them were playing instruments: violins, a cello, a French horn, and a trumpet. And one lady was playing one of two grand pianos in the room. The client described one of the men. He had a beard and was playing the violin. Then the dream shifted to a large white building.

As the woman continued with more details of her dream, Sharon realized she was describing the Majors' B&B, and the large, white building was the nearby Scottish Rite Masonic Temple.

After the session, Sharon took her client to the house. When they walked in and the woman saw the living room, she was stunned. This was the place she had seen in her dream, and looking at the pictures on the wall, she was even more amazed to see the bearded man. It was Edwin Northup. Edwin Northup was not only an engineer and musician, but also a Scottish Rite Freemason.

And for once, Sue and I had our own strange experiences. Around 2 A.M. the second night we were there, Sue woke up to the smell of tea brewing, a strong tea like Earl Grey or English Breakfast. She tiptoed downstairs to see who was up at that hour. Not a soul stirred. At breakfast that morning, she asked Barbee if anyone had been in the kitchen late making tea. Barbee assured her no one had been awake then.

Two nights later, at about three o'clock, I was awakened by a gentle but firm tug on my toe. I was lying on my back and someone or something had grabbed my toe. I sat straight up and looked around. I could see no one, and there was plenty of ambient light from the street outside. Sue lay breathing softly beside me, obviously in a deep sleep. I got up, checked the door, which was locked, and went into the bathroom, turning on the light. No one was there. When I mentioned the incident to Barbee in the morning, she laughed, "That's never happened before."

Looking at the Victorian Bed-and-Breakfast guest log, it's obvious that the inn is a way station not only for business people and tourists, but also for artists, musicians, and writers. So perhaps many of the occurrences that some think are paranormal are just the results of very creative, overactive imaginations. On the other hand . . . .

Spotlight on Old Christ Church

Old Christ Church on Adams Street in Historic Pensacola Village was built in 1832 and has had a colorful history. It was the Episcopal Church for Pensacola until the Civil War began. Confederate troops occupied Pensacola in 1861 and turned the church into a hospital for wounded soldiers.

In 1862 Union forces drove the rebels out. The Yankees continued using the church as a hospital, but also housed troops there and even had a jail in the building. Three priests, all rectors of the church before 1853, were buried in the nave in front of the chancel and altar. Allegedly, during the war, a boy saw Union soldiers dig up the graves of the priests, probably looking for valuables.

The story of this desecration was passed down through the decades. An old woman, a member of the parish, had supposedly talked to the boy who saw the soldiers digging. He was no longer alive, but the woman kept insisting that the story was true. Finally, through the efforts of Christ Church's rector, Dr. Currin, the University of West Florida conducted an archeological investigation to see if, in fact, the priests were actually buried where they were supposed to be, and the remains were temporarily moved to a house next door. After the investigation had been completed, the graves inside the church were restored and Dr. Currin conducted a funeral for the priests.

One of the students in the class that had conducted the investigation, Gary, watched as the funeral procession left the house and proceeded down the street to the church. He remembered the procession quite clearly: the crucifer, the choir, Dr. Currin, the president of the university, three clergymen dressed in white clerical vestments, and finally the pallbearers escorting the caskets. One of the clergymen in front of the pallbearers was carrying a black book, probably a Book of Common Prayer and was quite serious. The other two were laughing. When Gary looked at them more closely, he noticed that all three were barefoot, which he thought quite odd. After the procession wound its way down the street and around the fence into the churchyard, Gary lost sight of them, and he didn't see them in the church during the funeral. Even more oddly they did not show in any of the pictures that were taken of the proceedings.

CHAPTER 30

Seville Quarter
PENSACOLA

I WAS DEPRESSED. Sue and I had been in Pensacola, the last stop on our haunted road trip, for two days, and one of the stories I had come to research hadn't panned out. Sue, in her wisdom, suggested we stop for a glass of wine. It was only mid-afternoon, but, as if preordained, we found ourselves right in front of the Seville Quarter on Government Street. I couldn't argue with fate, so we popped into the enclosed alleyway between Rosie O'Grady's and Lili Marlene's.

In 1967, Bob Snow, an iconic Florida entrepreneur and show-man, opened Rosie O'Grady's Good Time Emporium in the old Pensacola Cigar Tobacco Company warehouse, which was built in 1871. With the Naval Air Station, the training center for hundreds of Navy and Marine Corps pilots, close by, Rosie's was an immediate success. Snow, himself an old Navy man, soon added six more clubs to the entertainment and dining complex. From Rosie O'Grady's to Phineas Phogg's Balloon Works on the opposite end of the establishment, the entire place provided entertainment for the whole family, from dancing or shooting pool to late night or even early morning dining.

In 1988, Mr. Snow encountered financial difficulties and the Mitchell family took over the complex, adding Heritage Hall, a beautiful banquet facility, and the Party Plaza, a large outdoor area used for open-air events and concerts.

Sue and I ambled down the cool, dark alleyway, deciding to explore before we sat down for our wine. On our right, Rosie's was dark and empty, but we could hear laughter and clacking billiard balls coming from the back bar of Lili Marlene's and Fast Eddie's. We wandered around, looking at the fantastic furnishings in the place. Most of the venues had pressed-tin ceilings. The various ornate bars came from England, Jacksonville, and Chicago. There were captain's chairs, pub tables, and benches from old London pubs. Mirrors were procured from Scotland. Oversized chairs in Lili Marlene's first sat in the Supreme Court of Massachusetts. Many of the chandeliers and light fixtures came from New Orleans, and the huge glass doors in Annie's once welcomed visitors to the old Ursuline Convent there. As one of the bartenders said, "We're more New Orleans than New Orleans." Whether or not that's true, Seville Quarter was charming.

We found ourselves once again in the alleyway between Rosie's and Lili Marlene's, talking about the ghosts there. I had done research and knew the place was haunted, and I had even stopped at some of the bars to ask the bartenders about paranormal activity. None of them knew very much. As we approached the doorway to Lili Marlene's, Sue was saying, "You've got to find someone who knows about this place." Just as we turned into Lili's, I caught movement out of the corner of my eye and looked back down the alley to see a woman wearing a bright red shirt with a Rosie O'Grady's logo on it.

I walked up and introduced myself. I told her that I was writing a book and was looking for ghosts. "Well, you've come to the right place. I'm Nancy Rodriquez, the administrative assistant here, and I can tell you lots of stories. Let me call my friend Pattie. She does our ghost tours and can tell you even more."

Sue and I went into the bar and finally had our glass of wine while we waited. Soon Nancy returned with Pattie Krakowski, owner of Pensacola History and Hauntings.

For the next couple of hours, the ladies regaled us with stories about Seville Quarter. The women's restroom upstairs at Rosie's is where Nancy saw her first ghost. Nancy is a member of the Krewe of Seville, an organization that participates in parades and balls during Carnival season (Mardi Gras), wearing different costumes each year, depending on the Carnival theme. This particular year, Krewe Seville was wearing romantic, Renaissance-style attire. Nancy was in the restroom upstairs trying on dresses. The door was propped open, since people were coming in and out. She was standing at the sink next to the door when out of the corner of her eye, she saw a woman enter. Thinking it was only someone bringing in another dress, Nancy casually turned to see who it was. The woman wore a "Gunne Sax" style of dress, with puffy sleeves from shoulder to elbow, and tightly fitting from elbow to wrist. Her dress was high-necked, white, and floor-length, and her hair was piled loosely on top of her head. "She looked like Jane Seymour's character in the 1980 movie, *Somewhere in Time*," Nancy recalled. Nancy made eye contact with the woman and was shocked to see her own reflection through the woman in the mirror on the far wall. The woman immediately evaporated.

Rhyan worked at the complex as a graphic designer. She was a student at the University of West Florida and came to Rosie's in the evenings. She loved her job and worked extra hours, often coming in early and staying late. One late afternoon when she was in the office by herself, she looked up to see a woman standing in front of Nancy's desk, which was directly across from hers. The woman was quietly standing there, looking down at the desk. Rhyan couldn't see her face because the woman was in profile and the sun was shining through the window behind her. Then she realized that she could see the sunshine and dust particles through the woman. Stunned, Rhyan immediately called her boss, Buck Mitchell.

Buck called Nancy. "Hey, my girl's freaking out. She thinks she's seeing a ghost."

When Nancy finally reached a breathless Rhyan, the girl related what had happened. She said that when she had called out to ask if she could help, the woman disappeared. Rhyan drew a picture of her. She was wearing a long dress with a Victorian-era winter cape, and this incident occurred in July. No one has ever seen the woman since, but some surmise she might have been a prostitute who worked in the bordello that many think existed for a time in that part of the building.

Perhaps the most famous ghost in Seville Quarter is Wesley Gibbs. His picture hangs on the wall in Rosie's. Wesley had been a stevedore working on the Pensacola docks, but had injured himself in the 1980s and was on disability. With time on his hands, Wesley began hanging out at Rosie's. He was there so often that the staff started joking with him, telling him he should just come work there. Eventually, the Mitchells hired him, and he became a "bar back," the person who supports the bartender by replenishing stock, refilling ice chests, cleaning up, and assisting whenever needed.

Wesley was a hard worker and was to be promoted to bartender. Late one evening after his very first shift as a barkeeper, another employee needed a case of beer and went into the cooler to get it. There sat Wesley on a keg, unable to move or speak. An ambulance took him to Sacred Heart Hospital, where he was pronounced dead on arrival. He'd suffered a major heart attack. Wesley was sorely missed at Rosie's. He was buried in the local cemetery, and the Mitchells closed the Quarter for the funeral.

But Wesley seems to prefer the nightlife at Rosie's to the quiet of the graveyard. He is seen there all the time. Stories abound. Once, a new employee went back to the cooler late at night while the staff was closing up. He saw a man walking in the hallway and, thinking he was a patron who hadn't left, called to him, "Hey, man, what are you doing here?" The man stopped, looked at him—and dissolved into thin air.

The employee blanched and raced back up to the bar, almost knocking over the bartender. "Hey, you look like you've seen a ghost," he joked.

The new man gasped, "Yes! Yes, I think I did!" The bartender led him over to the door, pointed up at one of the pictures and asked, "Did he look like that?" "Yup, that's him." "If that's who you saw, you just saw Wesley," the bartender assured him and went back to his work.

There are many ghostly happenings at the complex—lights turning on and off, music sound systems inexplicably turned on very loudly, chandeliers swinging, pictures falling off walls for no reason—but the Seville Quarter isn't a scary place. It's a wonderful spot in which to relax, listen to music, eat good food, and unwind. Sue and I spent the rest of the afternoon and early evening enjoying Nancy and Pattie's stories, and having another glass of wine. Then we were finally on our way.

But we returned the next morning. We weren't chasing ghosts this time, only refreshing ourselves in the Palace Café over cappuccinos and a plate of beignets.

CHAPTER 31

Pensacola Lighthouse
PENSACOLA

SUE AND I WERE NEARING THE END of our stay in Pensacola, and although we had been disappointed by failing to get one of the stories we had wanted, we had been able to replace it with the tale from the Victorian B&B. And in the process we had met Sharon Renae, who'd had many experiences at our final destination, the Pensacola Lighthouse. So, on the next-to-the-last morning of our stay, we drove over to the U. S. Naval Air Station in great anticipation.

The Pensacola Lighthouse is the oldest lighthouse on the Gulf Coast and is still in operation. The original lighthouse tower was built in 1824 on the site where the Navy Lodge is now located. It replaced a lightship, the *Aurora Borealis,* which had been anchored to mark the entrance to the Pensacola harbor. Because of the tower's low height, only thirty feet, and poor lighting, it was eventually replaced by a new lighthouse a half-mile to the west. The new facility, 191 feet above sea level, was lit on January 1, 1859.

The first keeper of the original lighthouse was a bachelor, Jeremiah Ingraham, who lived alone in a small cottage next to the tower. He quickly tired of his lonely life and married Michaela Penalber in 1826. Ingraham died in the lighthouse in 1840. Legend says Michaela murdered him. In any case, she remained as the light keeper until she died in 1855, when her son-in-law, Joseph Palmes, took over.

The keeper's job in the Pensacola Lighthouse was difficult and lonely, and not particularly stimulating. Until the light was automated in 1939, the light keeper had to pull weights on a clock mechanism to keep the lens rotating, much like an old-fashioned grandfather's clock. He or she also had to carry two forty-pound buckets of oil up the 177 steps to fuel the light, in addition to the daily chores of cleaning the tower and keeper's house, polishing the lens and the brass fittings, and maintaining records. The light keeper made many trips up and down the tower and was busy both day and night. The person in charge of the lighthouse was bound to it, day after day, month after month, year after year with little outside contact.

In 1861, at the beginning of the Civil War, Confederate troops occupied Fort Barrancas, where the lighthouse was located, with Federal troops at Fort Pickens on the barrier island just a mile away to the south. The opposing armies traded artillery fire, and the lighthouse and keeper's quarters were hit, but suffered little damage. The light had been extinguished already and the lens taken to Alabama and hidden. After the war, it was retrieved and reassembled.

From the very beginning, the Pensacola Lighthouse was wrought with problems. The tower and keeper's house were hammered by hurricanes and struck by lightning. The original tower was built on the site of burial grounds from which the remains of the deceased had not been removed. Also, the light keeper's quarters were probably used to house wounded and dying soldiers during the Civil War. Locals believe that for these reasons, the whole area is haunted.

But even in Keeper Palmes's day, the lighthouse, keeper's house, and the surrounding area were rumored to be plagued by the ghost of James Ingraham, which perhaps lends credence to his violent death. Apparently, Ingraham drank a good deal—and according to legend, he wasn't a very pleasant drunk. He often beat his wife and, some say, even his children. To this day, visitors report hearing laughing, crying, screaming, and moaning on tours of the facility.

Some also see strange objects flying around and wraith-like beings at windows. Others experience cold spots and smell pipe tobacco when no one in the area is smoking. Orbs are very common, too, and are often found in photographs taken of the tower and keeper's house, even daytime pictures. Many hear footsteps on the stairs of the tower when no one else is about. Some visitors report being touched by unseen hands.

Locked doors are found open. One worker recently went up to make repairs on a mechanism on the top level where the lens is located. The heavy metal door was locked, so he went back down to get the key. When he returned, the lock had been opened. No one else was in the tower. After he had made his repairs and gotten in his car to leave, he noticed that one of the windows about two thirds of the way up the tower was open. He went back inside to close it. After climbing up to the window, he found it shut. Back on the ground he looked up. And again the window was open.

Sharon Renae recounted that once as she was ascending the lighthouse tower, she saw a little boy of about five or six. He was dressed in a sailor suit and was huffing up the stairs. He had been ill, but he told her he was allowed to go up to the first landing and call to his father above that it was time to eat. Perhaps a light keeper's child?

One of Sharon's more chilling experiences concerns a light keeper and his wife, possibly Ingraham and Michaela. Sharon was sitting quietly in the keeper's bedroom and saw, as if a videotape was playing, a woman sitting on a bed, peeling an apple with a kitchen knife. Sharon could smell pipe or cigar smoke coming from the hallway. The "video" kept playing over and over. Some, including Sharon, believe an intoxicated Ingraham came into the room she saw in her vision and started beating his wife until she stabbed him.

Oddly, in the present keeper's bedroom, a blood stain permanently marks the floor, a reminder of the death and violence associated with the lighthouse. The floor, once covered with tile, has been refinished several times, and yet the stain remains. Many conjecture that the blood might have come from the two births that occurred in the house or from wounded Civil War soldiers. There is no recorded evidence either way.

The lighthouse has been featured on the TV program *Haunted Lighthouses of America* and is a popular tourist destination in Pensacola. It still shines its beacon of safety to mariners entering Pensacola Bay, but the Pensacola Lighthouse and its outbuildings also contain a dark side of inexplicable and mysterious happenings. Maybe it's the austere black-and-white color of the tower or the high, lonesome sound of the wind whispering through the pines surrounding the place, but I sensed a pervasive melancholy and sadness.

Sue and I walked down to the pristine beach one last time and wistfully looked back up at the stately lighthouse, knowing that, after all the months and miles, we had just completed our haunted road trip of Florida.

Ghosthunting
Travel Guide

AMERICA'S
HAUNTED ROAD TRIP

Visiting Haunted Sites

All the haunted sites in this book are open to the public, and most charge no fees. You may wish to have a meal or at least a drink in the bars and restaurants listed. Also, many of them are included on the ghost tours in the area. Especially for families, the ghost tours provide a fun, relaxed, and non-threatening way to experience paranormal activity. Don't forget to call ahead to make sure the site you want to visit is open, and make sure you call to make reservations for ghost tours, especially during tourist season.

The Keys and the South

The Conch Republic is a magical place, unique in the entire world. While the rest of the Keys abound with paranormal activity, I chose to include only five stories from Key West for logistical reasons. They're all within walking distance of each other and are close to the action downtown. Food, drink, and lodging. That's Key West, and that's the mix of sites I have included. All of the locations listed are available for paranormal investigations. Contact the site managers to make arrangements or call Brant Voss of the Original Ghost Tours of Key West, who is an excellent contact. (See Ghostly Resources section.)

La Concha   (866) 786-9205

Crowne Plaza La Concha Key West Hotel
430 Duval Street, Key West, FL 33040
www.laconchakeywest.com

Be sure to visit the rooftop bar to watch a sunset, but don't forget to watch a sunset from Mallory Square also, an experience never to be forgotten. La Concha is a great place to stay—right in the middle of the action. Reasonably priced, too.

Hard Rock Café   (305) 293-0230

313 Duval Street, Key West, FL 33040-6565
www.hardrock.com

The Hard Rock is just down the street from La Concha and a short distance from Mallory Square. After watching the sunset, come back to the Hard Rock for a late supper. Best to call for reservations. Paranormal investigations are welcomed but must be arranged beforehand.
    Open daily, 11 A.M.–late night (really late)

Captain Tony's Saloon   (305) 294-1838

428 Greene Street, Key West, FL 33040
www.capttonyssaloon.com

Captain Tony's is a legendary place, home of Sloppy Joe's during the Hemingway era. Captain Tony, deceased many years, became an icon in Key West, and the saloon is a must-visit site in Key West. With children, it's best to stop by during the day. Without them, the later the better. Paranormal investigators, Hemingway impersonators, and pink elephants are welcome any time. Check with the bartender for hours of operation; times can vary.

Audubon House & Tropical Gardens   (305) 294-2116

205 Whitehead Street, Key West, FL 33040-6522
www.audubonhouse.com

The Audubon House has a self-guided audio tour of the house and gardens and a variety of other activities, including art classes. It is also available for weddings and other events. Of course, it is one of the stops on local ghost tours.
    Open 9:30 A.M.–4:30 P.M. Admission: adults $10, students $6.50, children ages 6–11 $5, under age 6 free

Marrero's Guest Mansion (305) 294-6977

410 Fleming Street, Key West, FL 33040
www.marreros.com

Just around the corner from La Concha Hotel, the Marrero's Mansion is a nice, reasonably priced alternative to hotel accommodations, especially for those who like the homey atmosphere of a B&B or small inn. The Mansion is popular, so make reservations early.

South Florida covers the bottom of the state from the Atlantic to Gulf coasts. The Miami-West Palm Beach metropolis is perhaps the most densely populated region of Florida. Conversely, the western portion of south Florida, which includes the Everglades and the cattle country west and south of Lake Okeechobee, is the least populated. Both areas have much to offer. Visiting haunted sites in the south will take time, which might best be split between the east and the west. You might consider two separate trips, one to Miami to explore haunted sites, enjoy the night life, and participate in the myriad of daytime activities, and another to the Gulf Coast, where the pace is slower and geared more toward nature.

Historic Biltmore Hotel of Coral Gables   (305) 445-1926

1200 Anastasia Avenue, Coral Gables, FL 33134
www.lhwcom/biltmore

The Biltmore is located about three miles south of the Miami International Airport. Specific directions can best be obtained from an online map. Even if you don't stay there, the Biltmore is a must-see attraction in the Miami area.

Colony Hotel & Cabaña Club   (561) 276-4123

525 East Atlantic Avenue, Delray Beach, FL 33483-5323
www.thecolonyhotel.com

The Colony is right in the middle of all the action in quaint and colorful Delray Beach. There are dozens of great restaurants within walking distance, and the Colony has the Cabaña Club less than two miles away with a beautiful and private beach. If that's not enough, the ghosts at the Colony are very entertaining.

Riddle House   (561) 793-0333

9067 Southern Boulevard, West Palm Beach, FL 33411-3625
www.southfloridafair.com

Check Web site for hours of operation, events, and admission fees. Everyone should see the exhibits here for an excellent picture of the history of Florida. Visiting the Riddle House can also be exciting, especially if you meet the man on the stairs.

Arcadia's Old Opera House & Museum   (865) 494-3006

106 West Oak Street, Arcadia, FL 34266
Paula Rhodes-Zager, Proprietor

The upper floor of the Old Opera House & Museum is actually "The Shops
Upstairs," an eclectic antique mall within the Opera House and the most
haunted. It has been investigated several times, most often by Peace River
Ghost Tracker Paranormal Investigations. Scott Walker and Sprout Dvorak of
PRGT are more than willing to give tours of the site. Call ahead for hours of
operation; it's usually open from 10 A.M.–5 P.M.

West Central

Tampa is the second-largest metropolitan area in the state,
but there are many beautiful and lonely stretches between I-75
and the Gulf Coast. A day trip from Tampa Bay up along Route 19
to Cedar Key is well worth the drive. And, of course, the haunted
sites listed here are within easy reach, although you won't be
able to visit all of them in a day or even a weekend.

Redhawk Ranch   (813) 634-5352

Redhawk Ranch Spiritual Retreat
4110 CR 579 South, Wimauma, FL 33598
www.redhawkretreat.com
Bud and Brenda Hoshaw, owners

The Redhawk is a magical place, and Bud and Brenda are gracious hosts. Just
southeast of Tampa, it's a million miles from nowhere—but very easy to reach.
Take Exit 240A off I-75, east two miles on CR 674 to CR 579 in Wimauma, then
south five miles to the ranch. Call ahead, because the Hoshaws keep their gate
locked.

King Corona Cigars Café & Bar   (813) 241-9109

1523 East Seventh Avenue, Tampa, FL 33605
www.kingcoronacigars.com
Don Barco, Proprietor

In addition to the great ghost stories Don Barco and Joe Howden can tell you,
King Corona has a wonderful selection of cigars and also serves breakfast,
lunch, and dinner—everything with a Cuban accent.

Open Monday–Wednesday, 8 A.M.–midnight; Thursday, 8 A.M.–1 A.M.; Friday, 8 A.M.–2 A.M.; Saturday, 10 A.M.–2 A.M.; Sunday, noon–11 P.M.

Don CeSar Hotel   (727) 360-1881 or (800) 282-1116

3400 Gulf Boulevard, St. Petersburg Beach, FL 33706-4015
www.loewshotels.com

The Don CeSar is a magical place, not only because of the paranormal activity but also because of the beautiful setting and the service. It is conveniently located at the end of the Pinellas Bayway, a few minutes from I-275—but once there, guests are transported to another world. And most staff members will be only too willing to talk about the ghosts.

Tampa Theatre   (813) 274-8981

711 North Franklin Street, Tampa, FL 33602-4435
www.tampatheatre.org

The Tampa is a special and beloved place, as much a part of the city of Tampa as Ybor City and the Buccaneers. There are movies, concerts, and other special events every night of the year. Virtuoso organists play the Mighty Wurlitzer Thursdays, Fridays, Saturdays, and Sundays. And there are tours several times during the year. Private tours for small groups can also be arranged by calling the box office or e-mailing gargoyles@tampatheatre.org.

Box office hours: Monday–Friday, 10 A.M.–5 P.M.; evenings and weekends, between one-half hour before the first showtime of the day and one-half hour after the last showtime starts. When Tampa Theatre is presenting or hosting a concert or special event, box office hours will vary. Please call the box office at (813) 274-8286 to confirm box office hours for concerts or special events.

Admission fees vary depending upon the event. Call the box office to confirm hours and prices.

May-Stringer House   (352) 799-0129

601 Museum Court, Brooksville, FL 34601
www.hernandohistoricalmuseumassoc.com

The 150-year-old May-Stringer House is one of the most haunted places in Florida and also an excellent example of Victorian architecture in the area. With over ten thousand artifacts and so many ghosts, it is well worth a visit—day and night.

Open Tuesday–Sunday, noon–3 P.M. Call ahead to arrange for ghost tours and other special events. Admission: adults $5, children $2.

A Antique Mall   (352) 591-9588

17990 NW 77th Avenue, Reddick, FL 32686
www.aantiquefestival.com

It's hard to miss the huge yellow-and-black A Antique Mall sign on the west side
of I-75 at Exit 368 (CR 318). It's halfway between Gainesville and Ocala. Take the
exit west and then the first right (north) turn. Whether you like antiques or not,
it's worth a visit to see the place and listen to Warren Keene, the proprietor. He
is very entertaining.

Open Monday–Saturday, 10 A.M.–6 P.M., Sunday, noon–5 P.M.

East Central

There is more to east central Florida than Disneyworld, Sea
World, and Universal Studios—much, much more. Obviously,
the beaches are great, but we also have many places along the St.
John's River to explore, airboat rides, springs in which to swim
or view manatees, state and county parks, hiking trails. The pos-
sibilities are endless. And, we also have our ghosts. Orlando,
Daytona, New Smyrna, Cassadaga, to name just a few, have lots
of paranormal activity.

Orange County Regional History Center   (407) 836-8500

65 East Central Boulevard, Orlando, FL 32801
www.thehistorycenter.org

Located at the corner of Central and Magnolia and across the street from the
Orange County Library, the History Center is easy to find. The museum contains
three floors of outstanding displays on central Florida history.

Open daily, 10 A.M.–5 P.M. Call for information about ghost tours. Admission:
adults $12, military and seniors over age 60 $9, children ages 5–12 $7. Call to
check on group rates for parties of ten or more.

Longwood Village Inn   (407) 826-4000

300 N. Ronald Reagan Boulevard, Longwood, FL 32750
www.longwoodvillageinn.com; ann@homevest.com

The Longwood Village Inn is an office building, but it is on the National Register
of Historic Places and well worth a visit. Paranormal investigations may also be

arranged. It is easy to find. Take the Highway 434 Exit east to Ronald Reagan Boulevard, then drive north about one-quarter mile.

Page Jackson Cemetery

Sanford Cemetery, Sanford, FL 32773

The Page Jackson Cemetery is part of the Sanford Cemetery complex, which includes All Souls Catholic, Lakeview, and Evergreen Cemeteries in Sanford on West 25th Street about halfway between Florida 417 Toll (Exit 52) and US 17-92, approximately three-quarters of a mile either way. Page Jackson sits behind All Souls Catholic Cemetery and is privately owned. Paranormal investigations can be arranged, day or night, by calling Rich Cirone, Kissimmee Paranormal Investigations (407) 396-7776.

Pinewood Cemetery

Daytona Beach

Pinewood Cemetery is located on Peninsula between Main Street and Auditorium Boulevard, just off the Main Street Bridge. It is open to the public during daylight hours but closed at night. Tours can be arranged through Dusty Smith at the World's Most Famous Beach Ghost Tours at (386) 253-6034 or online at www.hauntsofdaytona.com.

North

North Florida is quite different from the rest of the state. From the accents of many there, you'd think you were in Georgia. Except for the Jacksonville area, it is quite rural. Hillier than central and south Florida, it is also blessed with sparkling beaches of its own on both the Gulf and Atlantic Coasts. And there is St. Augustine, oldest city in the nation, overrun by tourists of late but still a fascinating place, as well as one of the most haunted on the continent.

Spanish Military Hospital   (904) 827-0807 or (904) 827-0590

#3 Aviles Street, St. Augustine, FL 32084
www.ancientcitytours.net
ancientcitytours@bellsouth.net

The Spanish Military Hospital Museum provides a remarkable look into the lives of the Spanish who first settled St. Augustine in 1565 and occupied it until 1821, except for a brief twenty-year period in the 1700s when the British possessed the town. It is also incredibly haunted. In addition to the tours, paranormal investigations can be arranged through Diane Lane of Ancient City Hauntings.

Museum: Monday–Saturday, 10 A.M.–4:30 P.M.; Sunday, noon–4 P.M.; Ghost Tour: 8 P.M. nightly.

Museum Admission: adults $5, seniors $4.50, children ages 6–12 $3, children under age 6 free; Ghost Tour Fees: $12, children under age 6 free.

Ripley's Believe It or Not! Museum   (904) 824-1606

19 San Marcos Avenue, St. Augustine, FL 32084
www.staugustine.ripleys.com

Ripley's is located just north of the Castillo and is a must-see attraction in St. Augustine. There are thousands of really strange objects displayed. It's not called an "odditorium" for nothing.

Open: Sunday and Monday, 9 A.M.–7 P.M.; Friday and Saturday, 9 A.M.–8 P.M.

Ghost Tours: 8 P.M. nightly (Call for reservations, either at Ripley's or Ancient City Tours (904) 827-0807 or (904) 827-0590.)

Homestead Restaurant   (904) 247-6820

1712 Beach Boulevard, Jacksonville Beach, FL 32250
www.homesteadrestaurant.us

If you like chicken, you must go to the Homestead. And if you're a ghosthunter or you just like a good ghost story, the Homestead is a great place to visit. You might even get to meet Mrs. Paynter.

Open: Monday–Saturday, 4–10 P.M.; Sunday, 2:30–9 P.M.

The Amelia Island Williams House   (904) 277-2328

103 South Ninth Street, Fernandina Beach, FL 32034-3616
www.williamshouse.com

Fernandina Beach is a great weekend get-away destination, and the Williams House is the perfect place to stay. It's a short walk from the Williams to Centre Street and some wonderful shops, restaurants, and bars.

Olustee Battlefield   (386) 758-0400

Olustee Battlefield Historic State Park, US 90, Olustee, FL 32087

Olustee is the site of the biggest, bloodiest Civil War battle in Florida. In February there is a reenactment of the battle, as well as a festival with crafts, food, and demonstrations. Call (386) 755-1097 or (386) 758-1312. Trails lace the park and the Interpretive Center is excellent. Paranormal investigations can be arranged through the park headquarters.

Open: Battlefield: 8 A.M.–sunset daily. Interpretive Center: 9 A.M.–5 P.M. Admission: Free

The Panhandle

The Panhandle is perhaps my favorite region of Florida. It is less populated and more pristine than almost anywhere else in the state, and there are dozens of small towns that haven't been tainted much by modern life. Of course, there are many haunted places, too. As northeast Florida is more Georgia than Florida, so the Panhandle is Alabama through and through. The folks will quickly forgive you if you don't speak the "language." They're very friendly, even the ghosts.

Palmer House

Palmer House Antiques, 335 South Jefferson, Monticello, FL 32344

Monticello is the most haunted little town in the South, and you won't be disappointed with the evening ghost tour, which takes you to the Palmer House. The antiques are great, too.

Open: Tuesday–Saturday, 9 A.M.–5 P.M. Call Betty Davis, Big Bend Ghost Trackers, at (850) 508-8109 to arrange for ghost tours.

Knott House Museum   (850) 922-2459

301 East Park Avenue, Tallahassee, FL 32301-1513

Tallahassee, our state capitol, is a wonderful place to visit, and the Knott House Museum fits well into the stately decorum of the town. Paranormal investigations have been suspended for a time, but you might be able to arrange an investigation by visiting the museum and talking to the director.

Guided tours on the hour, Wednesday–Friday, 1, 2, and 3 P.M.; Saturday, 10 A.M., 11 A.M., noon, 1 P.M., 2 P.M., and 3 P.M.

Leaf Theatre   (850) 875-9444

The Quincy Music Theatre
118 E. Washington Street, Quincy, FL 32351
www.qmtonline.com; gmt@tds.net

The Quincy Music Theatre, housed in the old and haunted Leaf Theatre a
block off US 90 in Quincy, just west of Tallahassee, presents five or six major
productions each year in addition to several concerts. To visit the theater during
the day or to arrange a paranormal investigation, call Bill Mock, Managing
Director. Betty Davis and Lisa Guancial, (850) 508-8109, of the Big Bend Ghost
Trackers, are also willing to assist in making arrangements.

Coombs House Inn   (850) 653-9199 or (888) 244-8320

80 Sixth Street, Apalachicola, FL 32320
www.coombshouseinn.com

The Coombs House Inn is located in downtown Apalachicola just off US 98
(Chestnut Street) a few blocks west of the bridge in the historic district. The
inn has twenty-three rooms in two spectacular side-by-side mansions, both of
which have been painstakingly restored. Apalachicola is one of those kickback-
and-relax, out-of-the-way oases where you can really unwind. The staff at the
Coombs is extremely hospitable, as are the ghosts.

Pensacola Victorian Bed-and-Breakfast   (850) 434-2818

203 West Gregory Street, Pensacola, FL 32502
www.pensacolavictorian.com

Two blocks north of US 98 on the corner of Spring and Gregory in downtown
Pensacola, this homey, comfortable bed-and-breakfast has only four rooms and
provides an intimate atmosphere, as well as outstanding breakfasts. Next door,
Barbee and Chuck Major, the owners, also have a small café, The Cottage Café,
which is open for lunch.

Seville Quarter   (850) 434-6211

130 East Government Street, Pensacola, FL 32502
www.sevillequarter.com

Seville Quarter has been the premier entertainment center in Pensacola since
1967. There is fun there for the whole family day and night, and the ghost tour
is not only entertaining, but also very educational. Don't ask Wesley to make his
presence known, however—he just might!

The Palace Café opens at 6 A.M. weekdays, 7 A.M. Saturday, and 5 P.M. Sunday. The other rooms in the complex open at various times during the day beginning at 11 A.M. and close as late as 2:30 A.M.

Evening entertainment admission fees vary, depending on the event and the day. There is a ghost tour weekdays at 10:30 A.M. The cost is $24, which includes the tour, coffee, and lunch. Call Pattie Krakowski of Pensacola History and Hauntings (850) 221-1977.

Pensacola Lighthouse (850) 452-2749

Radford Boulevard, Pensacola, FL 32508
www.pensacolalighthouse.org

Entrance to the U.S. Naval Air Station is free. The lighthouse is a highlight of any visit to Pensacola, but also nearby is the National Museum of Naval Aviation. And if you time your visit right, you can see the U.S. Navy's Blue Angels practicing over the bay.

Check the calendar page on the Web site for operating hours. Opening and closing times vary. "Light of the Moon" ghost tours are conducted monthly from April through October. Check the calendar for dates and times.

Admission: Lighthouse tours, adults $5, children ages 7–11 $3. Ghost tour fees: call (850) 637-4050.

Ghostly Resources

Online Resources

There are literally thousands of Web sites pertaining to the paranormal, but these three were especially enlightening.

Ghosts: All About Ghosts

www.angelsghosts.com

This site provides all the information about ghosts anyone ever might want to know—history, theory, links, stories, anything and everything about ghosts.

International Ghost Hunters Society

www.ghostweb.com

Drs. Dave and Sharon Oester are the gurus of paranormal investigation. Their Web site offers information, photos, home-study courses, and a newsletter.

The Shadowlands

www.theshadowlands.net

This site provides a state-by-state, country-by-country index of ghost stories. A good place to start any paranormal research.

Books

I have fifteen or twenty of the dozens of books that have been written about Florida ghosts and paranormal activity. The following three were especially helpful as references.

Florida's Ghostly Legends and Haunted Folklore, Volumes 1, 2, and 3, by Greg Jenkins. Pineapple Press (2005, 2007, 2009).

The Florida Road Guide to Haunted Locations, by Chad Lewis and Terry Fisk. Unexplained Research Publishing Co. (2010)

Haunt Hunter's Guide to Florida, by Joyce Elson Moore. Pineapple Press. (1998)

Other Resources

These organizations were especially helpful to me in my research and have expressed a willingness to assist anyone desiring to explore the paranormal. Whether they are ghost tour groups or paranormal investigators, I can attest to their ethics and professionalism.

A Ghostly Encounter   (904) 827-0807 or (904) 827-0590

Diane Lane, President
3 Aviles Street, St. Augustine, FL 32084
ancientcitytours@bellsouth.net
www.ancientcitytours.net

Big Bend Ghost Trackers   (850) 508-8109

Betty Davis, President
P.O. Box 38141, Tallahassee, FL 32351
bbgt@BigBendGhostTrackers.com
www.BigBendGhostTrackers.com

Daytona Beach Paranormal Research Group, Inc.

Dusty Smith, Co-founder
Dusty@dbprginc.org
www.Dbprginc.org

Kissimmee Paranormal Investigations   (407) 396-7776

Rich Cirone, President
478 Greenwood Lane, Kissimmee, FL 34746
www.kissimmeeparanormal.com

The Original Key West Ghost Tours   (305) 294-9255, (305) 304-2208, or (305) 304-9341

Brant Voss, President
P.O. Box 4766, Key West, FL 33041
Brant@hauntedtours.com or Karen@hauntedtours.com
www.HauntedTours.com

Peace River Ghost Tracker Paranormal Investigations

Sprout Dvorak, Co-founder
Scott Walker, Co-founder
Preaceriverghosttracker@comcast.net
www.peaceriverghosttracker.com

Pensacola History and Hauntings   (850) 221-1977

Pattie Krakowski, President
130 East Government Street, Pensacola, FL 32502
pensacolahistoryandhauntings@cox.net
www.pensacolahistoryandhauntings.com

Pensacola Paranormal Society   (850) 469-0605

Sharon Renae, Co-founder
Sharon@sharonrenae.com
www.Sharonrenae.com
www.pensacolaparanormalsociety.com

Tampa Bay Ghost Watchers

Bill Sharpe, President
bill@tampabayghostwatchers.com
www.tampabayghostwatchers.com

West Florida Ghost Researchers

Rosemary Norman, Founder
rosemary@westfloridaresearchers.com
www.westfloridaghostresearchers.com

More Florida Haunts

Apalachicola: Gibson Inn, 51 Avenue C. Passersby hear the piano in the bar playing when the bar is closed.

Apalachicola: Orman House, 177 Fifth Street. The spirits of soldiers have been seen outside the museum.

Baker: Cobb Cemetery, Cobb Street. The ghost of a Ku Klux Klan member wanders the cemetery.

Boca Raton: Boca Raton Resort and Club, 501 E. Camino Real. A large white gull, believed to be the ghost of a pirate, dives at people who venture too near a large, old tree on the property.

Cassadaga: Cassadaga Hotel, 355 Cassadaga Road. Phantom voices can be heard throughout the second floor, and the spirit of a young girl plays tricks on the guests.

Crestview: Jameson Inn, 151 Cracker Barrel Drive. The elevator sometimes goes into operation even when it is empty and no one has pushed any buttons.

Daytona Beach: Daytona Playhouse, 100 Jessamine Boulevard. The spirits of a nattily dressed man and woman are seen together throughout the theater.

Delray Beach: Blue Anchor Pub, 804 East Atlantic Avenue. The ghost of Bertha Starkey, who was stabbed to death by her husband, haunts the pub.

Delray Beach: Delray Beach Playhouse, 950 NW Ninth Street. The spirit of Bob Blake, the founder and architect of the playhouse, is often seen on stage.

Fernandina Beach: Bosque Bello Cemetery, North 14th Street. Numerous apparitions, including three children, haunt the site.

Fernandina Beach: Florida House Inn, 22 South Third Street. Glowing red eyes have been seen in the kitchen window.

Fernandina Beach: Fort Clinch, 2601 Atlantic Avenue. Ghosts of Civil War soldiers are seen in the courtyard.

Fernandina Beach: Old Jail, 233 South Third Street. Ghost of pirate Luc Simone Aury haunts the jail.

Fernandina Beach: Palace Saloon, 117 Centre Street. Patrons and staff see the spirit of Uncle Charlie throughout the bar.

Fort Pierce: Boston House, 239 Indian River Drive. Aleacon Perkins wanders the building at night, waiting for her lost son to return.

Hobe Sound: Jonathon Dickinson State Park, 16450 SE Federal Highway. The ghost of Trapper Nelson has been seen roaming the park.

Hollywood: Hollywood Beach Resort, 101 North Ocean Drive. The ghosts of two murder victims prowl the seventh floor.

Jenson Beach: Leach Mansion, 1701 NE Indian River Drive. Disembodied lights swirl around the property.

Jupiter: Jupiter Inlet Lighthouse, Lighthouse Park, 500 Captain Armour's Way. Shadowy apparitions roam the grounds at night.

Key West: Artist's House, 534 Eaton Street. The ghost of a woman glides through the house.

Key West: Hemingway House, 907 Whitehead Street. Hemingway's ghost is seen walking from his second-floor bedroom to his studio, where a catwalk used to run.

Key West: St. Paul's Episcopal Church, 401 Duval Street. Apparitions are seen in the church graveyard.

Key West: Club Chameleon, Truman Avenue and White Street. Screams of children who died in a fire in the building can be heard on the street outside.

Lake Helen: Lake Helen-Cassadaga Cemetery, corner of Kicklighter Road and Macy Avenue. Apparitions seen throughout the cemetery.

Lake Wales: Spook Hill, North Wales Drive. Cars roll uphill and road is allegedly haunted by a ghost alligator.

Lake Worth: Lake Worth Playhouse, 713 Lake Avenue. Two brothers who both committed suicide in the theater now meander through the place.

Miami: Anderson's General Store, 15700 SW 232nd Street. The screams of a young woman physically abused by her stepfather can be heard.

Miami: Villa Paula, 5811 North Miami Avenue. The angry ghost of a woman who died mysteriously in the villa haunts the place.

Miami Springs: Glenn H. Curtiss Mansion, 500 Deer Run. Unearthly screams resound throughout the neighborhood.

Monticello: John Denham House, 555 West Palmer Mill Road. Aunt Sarah stalks the hallways.

Ocala: Seven Sisters Inn, 828 SE Fort King Street. Lizzy tucks the guests in at night.

Oklawaha: Ma Barker's House, East Highway 25. The ghost of Ma Barker peers out the window.

Orlando: Ceviche Restaurant, 125 West Church Street. The ghost of a woman appears in the mirror behind the bar.

Orlando: Greenwood Cemetery, 1603 Greenwood Street. Shadowy apparitions wander the grounds at night.

Orlando: Leu Gardens, 1920 North Forest Avenue. Ghosts of two women have been seen on the veranda of the Leu House Museum.

Orlando: Rouse Cemetery, Rouse Road. An angry spirit stalks anyone who enters after dark.

Panama City: Holiday Inn, 11127 West Highway 98. The ghost of a decapitated young man appears at 4 A.M.

Palm Beach: Flagler Museum, 1 Whitehall Way. A ghost of an unknown person stares out a second-floor window.

Pensacola: Dorr House, 311 South Adams Street. Misty figures are seen moving through the house.

Port Charlotte: Restlawn Memorial Gardens, 1380 Forest Nelson Boulevard. A ghostly apparition wanders through the cemetery at night.

Port St. Lucie: The Devil's Tree, Oak Hammock Park, 1982 SW Villanova Road. The spirits of two young women sexually assaulted, murdered, and hanged from the tree now haunt the area.

Quincy: Allison House, 215 North Madison Street. Guests have seen the ghosts of former governor A.K. Allison and his daughter, Sarah, wandering through the inn.

Rockledge: Ashley's Café & Lounge, 1609 US Highway 1. The apparition of a young woman wanders around the restaurant.

Sebring: Harder Hall, 3300 Golfview Road. Dark, shadowy apparitions wander the halls.

St Petersburg: Vinoy Resort, 501 Fifth Avenue NE. A top-hatted apparition roams the grounds at night.

St Petersburg: Haslam's Bookstore, 2025 Central Avenue. Ghost of Jack Kerouac allegedly haunts the store.

Tallahassee: Velda Mound Park, Arbor Hill. The ghost of a white wolf howls in the middle of the night.

Tampa: David Falk Theatre, 428 West Kennedy Boulevard. The spirit of deceased actress Bessie Snavely haunts the theater.

Tampa: Myrtle Hill Memorial Park, 4207 East Lake Avenue. Women's screams are heard throughout the cemetery.

Tarpon Springs: Rose Historical Cemetery, North Jasmine Avenue and East Orange Street. Spirits of deceased wander in the cemetery waiting for proper burials.

Wauchula: Bloody Bucket Bridge, Bridge Road. The river turns red with the blood of babies murdered by a deranged midwife.

Acknowledgments

FIRST, I WOULD LIKE TO THANK my editor, John Kachuba, for his guidance and encouragement. Many thanks, too, to all the wonderful folks at Clerisy Press. It's a great publishing house to work with.

I am also grateful beyond words for all the many, many people who helped me with the stories. In particular, I want to thank Cynthia Anderson, Don Barco, Pierce Berg, Ann Bierdenharn, Claire Castillo, Rich and Kim Cirone, Wendi Davis, Betty Davis, Louie Deguin, Mandy Dunn, Sprout Dvorak, Don Estep, Lisa Guancial, Tom Hambright, Susan Harrell, Lee Holloway, Bud and Brenda Hoshaw, Joe Howden, Ralf Ingwersen, Warren Keene, Patti Krakowski, Diane Lane, Lois Lee, Steve Mackiewcz, Barbee Major, Casey McCarthy, Cynthia Melendez, Robert Merritt, Terri-Anne Miller, Bill Mock, Amanda Mullen, Rosemary Norman, Niki Padron, Dr. Tana Porter, Sharon Renae, Paula Rhoads-Zager, Nancy Rodriguez, Dusty Smith, Bill Spohrer, Sheila Steen, Minda Stephens, Frank and Debbie Visicaro, Pete Vosotas, Brant Voss, Scott Walker, Destinee Welch, and Lynn Wilson Spohrer. If I've missed anyone, I apologize. I also owe my ghosthunting pal, Joanne Maio, and her daughters, Gwyneth and Miranda, a huge debt of gratitude for all their help.

I also relied heavily on Florida's *Ghostly Legends and Haunted Folklore*, Volumes 1, 2, and 3, by Greg Jenkins, Pineapple Press (2005, 2007, 2009); *The Florida Road Guide to Haunted Locations*, by Chad Lewis and Terry Fisk. Unexplained Research Publishing Co. (2010); and *Haunt Hunter's Guide to Florida*, by Joyce Elson Moore. Pineapple Press. (1998) as references. All ghosthunters should have these three volumes in their libraries.

And finally, I must thank my spouse, my first reader, my severest critic, and my muse, Sue. She makes me look good.

About the Author

DAVE LAPHAM is a retired Marine officer and the author of the best-selling books *Ghosts of St. Augustine,* and *Ancient City Hauntings.* He has also published numerous magazine articles and appeared in television documentaries and on radio. He lives with his wife, Sue, and dog, Buddy, in Orlando, Florida, where he has continued his writing career with this third collection of ghost stories. He is currently working on a novel—and, yes, it has ghosts.

Printed in the USA
CPSIA information can be obtained
at www.ICGtesting.com
JSHW012025140824
68134JS00033B/2871